The New
AMERICAN
REVOLUTION
Handbook

Facts and Artwork for Readers of All Ages

Theodore P. Savas

and J. David Dameron

Savas Beatie
New York and California

Cataloging-in-Publication Data is available from the Library of Congress.

ISBN 978-1-932714-93-7

05 04 03 02 01 5 4 3 2
First edition, second printing

SB

Published by
Savas Beatie LLC
521 Fifth Avenue, Suite 1700
New York, NY 10175

Editorial Offices:

Savas Beatie LLC
P.O. Box 4527
El Dorado Hills, CA 95762
Phone: 916-941-6896
(E-mail) editorial@savasbeatie.com

Savas Beatie titles are available at special discounts for bulk purchases in the United States by corporations, institutions, and other organizations. For more details, please contact Special Sales, P.O. Box 4527, El Dorado Hills, CA 95762, or you may e-mail us at sales@savasbeatie.com, or visit our website at www.savasbeatie.com for additional information.

Cover Art: *Guilford Courthouse, 15 March 1781,* by H. Charles McBarron, Jr. United States Army Center of Military History (CMH) Publication 70-5, "Soldiers of the American Revolution."

To my wife Carol and my children, Demetrious Theodore and Alexandra Maria.
I love you all more than you will ever know.

— Theodore P. Savas

To my wife Pamela and my children, Kevin Michael and Christina Leigh.
You are my heart and soul—always.
— J. David Dameron

Contents

Contents (continued)

Foreword

Colonial America and the Revolution have fascinated us both for as long as we can remember. Does not the soul stir when reading about the passions that prompted men to risk everything they owned to throw off the bonds of tyranny to embark on an experiment uncharted in human history? Does not the blood in one's veins flow faster when walking across Concord Bridge or standing before the redoubts at Yorktown while imagining the courage and tenacity necessary to face down the most mightiest army in the world? Does not peering over the shoulders of the men who penned the Declaration of Independence and later crafted our remarkable Constitution—two founding documents that have helped spread freedom around the world to untold millions—instill pride and a sense of decency?

A lingering misconception confines the War for American Independence to a handful of battles in New England. Although the war did indeed break out on Lexington Green in April 1775, the conflagration spread quickly north into Canada, west into Indian Territory, south into the Carolinas, and across the seas into a massive global conflict that pulled in several other countries and would not leave even the British home islands unscathed.

As it is with any major war, learning about the American Revolution is always a bit problematic. Few people have the time or inclination to read full-length books on the subject. Unfortunately, introductory studies and materials available to most students often focus on a thin handful of well-known engagements and personalities. The result leaves an impression that the Revolution was a limited war—and by implication a subject worth only brief study. Nothing could be further from reality.

We teamed up to write *A Guide to the Battles of the American Revolution* (2005) in an effort to dispel this false notion. The *Guide* sets forth the organizations of the armies and all the major (and most of the minor) actions in a clear and organized formula that was easy to read and understand. Each entry was accompanied by an original map of the campaign/battle (most of which had never been mapped to any great extent, if at all). Our hope was that readers would more easily grasp how widespread the fighting really was, and that the American Revolution had a major impact on the course of Western society.

The New American Revolution Handbook explores similar themes, but goes well behind our prior work by introducing readers to a wide variety of aspects that were not suitable for inclusion in *A Guide to the Battles of the American Revolution*. Topical coverage includes organizations, the history of the key combatants, and a sizeable section on the fighting, but also includes subjects as diverse as women in the war, the role of Native Americans and African Americans, technology, voices of the war, and much more. It concludes with recommendations for more detailed research, a list of places to visit, and the Revolutionary War on the Internet. Experienced readers will readily identify the value of ship lists, organizational charts, and other detailed information.

It is our hope *The New American Revolution Handbook* will serve as a useful tool for teachers, students, and parents alike. As a quick fact reference book or as a leisure read, it will provide hours of exploration and immersion into a fascinating world at war that continues to impact our lives today.

*   *   *

Acknowledgments

The material presented in *The New American Revolution Handbook* was obtained from a variety of sources, including light archival research, autobiographies, and standard secondary studies about the war and its leaders. Unless otherwise noted, illustrations are courtesy of the National Archives and Library of Congress.

Jerry and Jean Dameron reviewed the material for general readership, flow, and interest. Pamela Dameron provided insightful perspectives regarding the "Women," "Indians,", and "Did You Know?" sections, while Melanie Crain and Michelle Patton, whose expertise in younger reader audiences provided invaluable insights from an educational perspective. Each of them gave freely of their time and encouraged us throughout the development process. We thank you all.

The helpful people at Savas Beatie made the publication process an enjoyable one. Editor Terry Johnston offered many valuable suggestions and helped develop the original structure of this book. Sarah Keeney, Savas Beatie's marketing director, offered insight along the way, as did Veronica Kane and Kim Rouse.

Finally, our wives and families are always supportive of our efforts that must, by necessity, take us away from them and our time together.

— Theodore P. Savas and J. David Dameron

Naming the War

From the opening of musket fire on Lexington Green down to the present day, different names have been assigned to the conflict waged between 1775 to 1783. While by no means comprehensive, the following list contains, in no particular order, the most popular among them.

British Names

The American War of Independence

The American Rebellion

The War of American Independence

The American War for Independence

The American Revolution

The Colonial Uprising

American Names

The American Revolution

The Rebellion

The Revolutionary War

The American War of Independence

The Great Rebellion

Voices of the American Revolution

"They that can give up essential liberty to purchase a little temporary safety deserve neither liberty nor safety."

— Benjamin Franklin, 1759

"Then join hand in hand, brave Americans all; By uniting we stand, by dividing we fall!"

— John Dickenson, 1768 (final verse of "The Liberty Song")

"There is a time for all things, a time to preach and a time to pray, but those times have passed away. There is a time to fight, and that time has now come."

— Rev. Peter Muhlenberg, January 1776

"Is life so dear or peace so sweet as to be purchased at the price of chains and slavery? Forbid it, Almighty God. I know not what course others may take, but as for me, give me liberty or give me death!"

— Patrick Henry, 1775

"Proclaim liberty throughout the land unto all the inhabitants thereof."

— Holy Bible, Leviticus 25:10 (Liberty Bell Inscription)

"We must all hang together, or assuredly we shall all hang separately."

— Benjamin Franklin, 1776

"These are the times that try men's souls. . . . What we obtain too cheap, we esteem too lightly; it is dearness only that gives everything its value."

— Thomas Paine, 1776

"Issue the orders, Sir, and I will storm hell!"

— Anthony Wayne, 1779, in reply to Gen. Washington's query regarding the British stronghold at Stony Point

"Don't fire unless fired upon, but if they mean to have a war, let it begin here."

— Command by Captain John Parker in April 1775 as British approached Lexington

"The hour is fast approaching, on which the honor and success of this army, and the safety of our bleeding country depend. Remember officers and soldiers, that you are free men, fighting for the blessings of liberty—that slavery will be your portion, and that of your posterity, if you do not acquit yourselves like men."

— Gen. George Washington, 1776

"Don't fire until you see the whites of their eyes! Then fire low!"

— Gen. Israel Putnam, 1776

"I have not yet begun to fight!"

— John Paul Jones, 1779, in response to the enemy's demand to surrender

"Yonder are the Hessians. They were bought for seven pounds and tenpence a man. Are you worth more? Prove it. Tonight the American flag floats from yonder hill or Molly Stark sleeps a widow!"

— Col. John Stark, 1777

"The house shakes . . . with the roar of the cannon. No sleep for me tonight."

— Abigail Adams, 1776

"What a glorious morning for America!"

— Samuel Adams, 1775, speaking about the first shots fired at Lexington and Concord

"Yesterday the greatest question was decided . . . and a greater question perhaps never was nor will be decided among men. A resolution was passed without one dissenting colony, that these United Colonies are, and of right ought to be, free and independent states."

— John Adams, 1776

"Driven from every other corner of the earth, freedom of thought and the right of private judgment in the matters of conscience direct their course to this happy country as the last asylum."

— Samuel Adams, 1776

"The war has actually begun! The next gale that sweeps from the north will bring to our ears the clash of resounding arms!"

— Gen. Nathanael Greene, 1781

"I never saw such fighting since God made me. The Americans fought like demons."

— Lord Charles Cornwallis, 1781, regarding the Battle of Guilford Courthouse

"I only regret that I have but one life to lose for my country."

— Nathan Hale, 1776 (before the British hanged him)

"There, I guess King George will be able to read that."

— John Hancock, 1776, after signing his name to the Declaration of Independence

"Our properties within our own territories [should not] be taxed or regulated by any power on earth but our own."

— Thomas Jefferson, 1774

"The die is now cast; the colonies must either submit or triumph. . . . We must not retreat."

— King George III, 1774

"Patriotism is as much a virtue as justice, and is as necessary for the support of societies as natural affection is for the support of families."

— Benjamin Rush, 1773, influential doctor and "Founding Father" from Pennsylvania

"Nevertheless, to the persecution and tyranny of his cruel ministry we will not tamely submit—appealing to Heaven for the justice of our cause, we determine to die or be free."

— Joseph Warren, 1775, influential doctor, patriot, and a leader of the Sons of Liberty

"The committee met, discussed the subject [of the Declaration of Independence] and then appointed Mr. Jefferson and me [John Adams] to make the draught, I suppose because we were the two first on the list. The subcommittee met. Jefferson proposed to me to make the draught.
Adams: I will not.
Jefferson: You should do it.
Adams: Oh no!
Jefferson: Why will you not? You ought to do it.
Adams: I will not.
Jefferson: Why?
Adams: Reasons enough.
Jefferson: What can be your reasons?

Adams: Reason first, you are a Virginian, and a Virginian ought to appear at the head of this business. Reason second, I am obnoxious, suspected and unpopular. You are very much otherwise. Reason third, you can write ten times better than I can.

Jefferson: Well if you are decided, I will do as well as I can.

Adams: Very well. When you have drawn it up, we will have a meeting."

— John Adams, 1776

"Nothing short of independence, it appears to me, can possibly do. A peace on other terms would . . . be a peace of war."

— Gen. George Washington, 1778

"I hope you will not consider yourself as commander in chief of your own house—but be convinced . . . that there is such a thing as equal command."

— Lucy Knox, 1777, in a letter to her husband Henry, Washington's chief of artillery

"We have not raised armies with ambitious designs of separating from Great Britain, and establishing independent states. We fight not for glory or for conquest."

— Second Continental Congress, 1776

"We hold these truths to be self-evident, that all men are created equal, that they are endowed by their Creator with certain unalienable Rights, that among these are Life, Liberty and pursuit of Happiness: that to secure these rights, governments are instituted among men, deriving their just powers from the consent of the governed."

— Declaration of Independence, 1776

"One if by land, two if by sea."

— Paul Revere, 1775 (signal for his Midnight Ride regarding approach of the British)

"With hearts fortified with these animating reflections, we most solemnly, before God and the world, declare, that, exerting the utmost energy of those powers, which our beneficent Creator hath graciously bestowed upon us, the arms we have compelled by our enemies to assume, we will, in defiance of every hazard, with unabating firmness and perseverance employ for the preservation of our liberties; being with one mind resolved to die freemen rather than to live as slaves."

— John Dickinson and Thomas Jefferson, 1775 (*Declaration of the Cause and Necessity of Taking up Arms*)

"There is not a single instance in history in which civil liberty was lost, and religious liberty preserved entire. If therefore we yield up our temporal property, we at the same time deliver the conscience into bondage."

> — John Witherspoon, 1776, influential "Founding Father" from New Jersey

"They came three thousand miles and died,
To keep the past upon its throne;
Unheard, beyond the ocean tide,
Their English mother made her moan."

> — Inscription on the grave of British soldiers that perished at Concord Bridge

"Liberty, when it begins to take root, is a plant of rapid growth."

> — Gen. George Washington, 1788

"Such firing never was heard in America. You would have thought Heaven and Earth were coming together."

> — Jacob Smith, soldier, writing in his journal about the fighting at Yorktown

"Pray led me hear when there is a probability of drawing clothing for the soldiers—they are very naked and are get'g sickly."

> — Colonel Charles Dabney, 1st Virginia State Military Regiment

"The Commanding Officer is astonished, that altho' he has repeatedly Issues Orders, to prevent the Soldiers' Wives selling Rum, the practice is still continued."

> — Colonel John Lamb, 2nd Artillery Regiment

"The British bayonet was repeatedly tried ineffectually."

> — British General John Burgoyne, writing about the fighting at Freeman's Farm

Did You Know?
Interesting Facts About the American Revolution

Contrary to popular belief, George Washington did not have wooden teeth. On January 27, 2005, researchers at the National Museum of Dentistry in Baltimore, Maryland, announced that laser scans of Washington's dentures indicate they were made of gold, ivory, and lead, and human, horse, and donkey teeth.

Everyone knows that America's birthday is celebrated on the 4th of July, but should it be July 2? The Continental Congress formally voted and agreed to declare independence from Great Britain on July 2, 1776. "Independence Day" was first declared on July 4, 1776—the date Congress agreed to the wording and published broadsides of the document for dissemination throughout the states. The original document on display in Washington, D.C. states July 4, 1776, but several of the signers did not actually affix their signatures until its formal adoption on August 2, 1776.

British General Lord Charles Cornwallis surrendered his army to General George Washington after losing the Siege of Yorktown on October 19, 1781. The American Revolution, however, did not formally end until the Treaty of Paris was signed nearly two years later on September 3, 1783. Fighting continued elsewhere during that time, and British troops did not leave American soil until November 25, 1783.

American militiamen fired the first shots of the Revolutionary War at Lexington Green on June 19, 1775. During the next few years the war expanded around much of the globe. France officially allied itself with the Americans on February 6, 1778, Spain joined the allegiance on April 12, 1779, and on December 20, 1780, Great Britain declared war on the Netherlands for secretly aiding the Americans.

According to military casualty records and medical reports, some 15,000 men on all sides died in battle, but 97,000 men died from disease.

Hessians (Germans) fought with the British as troops for hire during the war. These professional soldiers were respected throughout the world for their military abilities. According to official records, German princes deployed 29,867 men to support British operations on American soil, but only 17,313 returned home.

A British expedition was conducted in what is today Nicaragua from April 1780 through January of 1781. The British spent months besieging the Spanish at Fort San Juan before disease and death weakened their army and forced them to retreat. The effort cost the British at least 2,500 deaths from dysentery, yellow fever, malaria, and other tropical illnesses. Among the survivors was 21-year-old Captain Horatio Nelson, who would go on to become one of the most famous sea captains in history. Nelson, however, suffered for the rest of his life with bouts of malaria and other maladies contracted during his time spent in Nicaragua.

The liberal minority in Great Britain's parliament was against the war and argued unsuccessfully in favor of granting Americans their independence. In particular, Edmund Burke repeatedly warned against heavy-handed tactics in the colonies. In response to increased taxes, Burke warned the King in 1775 that the Americans would "cast your sovereignty in your face. No body of men will be argued into slavery." Ultimately, Burke's predictions became reality.

Many people have heard that King George III was "mad." Throughout his life, the King behaved erratically and suffered from serious bouts of depression and delirium. He was institutionalized and removed from the throne—but not until many years after the American Revolution.

Prior to the Revolution, Great Britain heavily taxed or restricted trade in the American colonies. Just about everything (from hats, sugar, molasses, wool, textiles, ink, coffee, tea, hides, lead, glass, paint, silk, soap, rum, tea, paper) was taxed. The costs and regulations angered the colonists, and were two of the reasons that helped bring about the war.

Prior to the Revolution, John Adams was an attorney. In fact, he defended the British soldiers who killed five people during the infamous "Boston Massacre" several years before the war broke out. His legal skills are reflected in the soldiers' acquittals at trial. Adams's desire to see justice prevail is admirable given the fact that the victims were found at fault for instigating the resulting bloodshed.

On the evening of December 16, 1773, 150 local Bostonians dressed as Indians boarded three British ships laden with valuable tea packed inside 342 chests. In an act of protest against what they deemed were oppressive British policies, the men dumped the entire cargo into the harbor. Its value today would be nearly 1.8 million dollars. The incident got the King's attention, and its relevance echos through time to this very day.

Historians estimate that nearly one-third of all American colonists wished to remain under British rule and so refused to join the revolt, another third remained neutral, and the remaining third actively sought independence. At least 25,000 men formed Loyalist Provincial American or "Tory" units and fought for the British against the Patriots.

At least 10,000 Indians aligned themselves with the British and waged war against Patriot settlers on the American frontier (Tennessee, Ohio, Mohawk, and Mississippi Valleys).

Several historians argue that had foreign allies (France, Spain, and the Netherlands) not joined the American cause, the British would have won the war. Without French naval assistance, the British navy would have dominated the seas, and without the Spaniards, the British would have controlled the southern and western territories (Florida and Mississippi).

At least 10,000 French died while fighting the British, and three-fourths (75%) of them lost their lives at sea. The Spanish lost 5,000 men while fighting the British, and another American ally, the Dutch, lost about 500 men.

France, Spain, and the Netherlands provided America with the bulk of its financing in terms of loans, grants, and war materiel.

During the Revolution, the first documented case of submarine warfare occurred when the Americans launched *The Turtle* against British ships anchored in New York harbor. The attempt was unsuccessful.

Lt. Colonel Daniel Boone's son Israel was killed at the Battle of Blue Licks (modern-day Kentucky) on August 19, 1782.

You can no longer visit the battlefield near Boston's Hog and Noodle Islands because the area is today comprised of landfills, reshaped by urban growth, and is better known as East Boston and Logan International Airport.

The October 7, 1780, Battle of King's Mountain, included several thousand combatants but only one soldier was a British regular officer: Major Patrick Ferguson, the commander of the Loyalists militia. Ferguson was killed during the combat.

Benedict Arnold is today best known as a traitor, but during the war he was considered one of the finest military officers on either side. He led men in battle on land, commanded a makeshift naval force at the Battle of Valcour Island, and served as a general on both sides (American and British).

The Dutch Island of St. Eustatius was the first foreign entity to formally acknowledge the American navy with a military salute. On November 16, 1776, the American Brig-of-war *Andrew Doria* pulled into port there and was warmly received with full military honors.

On September 5, 1781, the most important naval battle of the Revolution was waged off the coast of Virginia in what is now known as the Battle of the Capes. The French victory over the British secured the Chesapeake Bay and cut off the British land forces at Yorktown, where General Cornwallis ultimately surrendered his army.

The largest naval battle of the Revolutionary War was fought in the Caribbean along the Dominican coast between French and British fleets on April 12, 1782. Known today as the Battle of the Saints, 36 British ships of the line squared off against a French fleet of 33 warships. The French ran out of ammunition and lost 3,000 men killed and another 5,000 prisoners. The French commander, Admiral de Grasse, surrendered his flagship *Le Ville de Paris*, the pride of the French fleet, to the British along with 27 other warships. The stunning victory decimated the French navy and allowed the British to dominate the Caribbean for many years.

On March 3, 1776, the tiny American navy and its Marines attacked and seized British forts at Nassau in the Bahamas. The American victory gained vast stores of gunpowder (and rum) for the war effort back home.

After seizing a British schooner on Lake Champlain near Whitehall, New York, American army Colonel Benedict Arnold launched a series of naval raids in May of 1775 that resulted in the capture of four British ships (including a 70-ton sloop) and the destruction of five others. The victory secured control of Lake Champlain and marks the unofficial formation of the first American naval force in U.S. history. The United States Navy was not formally created by authorization of Congress until October 13, 1775.

One of General Washington's most dramatic and successful battles occurred after crossing the frozen Delaware River on Christmas Day and attacking the unsuspecting Hessians at Trenton, New Jersey. Nearly 1,500 Hessians were captured, wounded, or killed while American losses were just a dozen. One of the wounded Americans was a young lieutenant named James Monroe, who suffered from a severed artery. He survived both his wound and the war to become the fifth President of the United States on March 4, 1817.

Militarily significant battles were fought in the Northern colonies during the war, but large sieges and trapped armies in the South resulted in the largest losses. On May 12, 1780, American commander Major General Benjamin Lincoln surrendered the town of Charleston and the bulk of the Southern Department of the United States Army to the British. Lincoln's casualties numbered 226 killed and wounded and 6,684 prisoners, making the Siege of Charleston the largest single loss suffered by the Americans during the war. However, on October 18, 1781, British commander General Lord Charles Cornwallis lost nearly 500 men in battle and became trapped on the Yorktown peninsula of Virginia. Cornwallis surrendered his entire army of 7,177 men, making it the greatest single loss during the war and the most consequential.

Although fought thousands of miles from the United States, the Spanish and French siege of British-held Gibraltar was by far the longest and most expensive combat waged during the Revolutionary War. The protracted and unsuccessful siege lasted from three years and seven months (June 24, 1779

– February 7, 1783), but the British were able to maintain control of their stronghold (known as the "Rock of Gibraltar"). Both sides spent fortunes in terms of men, materiel, and money waging a series of battles that resulted in more than 8,000 casualties.

American Indians referred to General George Washington as "Conotocaurious," which translates as "Town Destroyer." This title refers to the destruction of Indian villages during the American Revolution. Nonetheless, after the war, Handsome Lake, a Seneca Indian religious chief, declared that President Washington would be the only white man allowed into Indian heaven. As the old saying goes, "Time heals all wounds."

History records that Alexander Hamilton, Washington's aide-de-camp, was a brave patriot and forthright officer during the American Revolution. Hamilton was born on the Caribbean island of Nevis, the identity of his father is unknown, and his actual birth date remains a mystery. Despite a difficult childhood, Hamilton rose to prominence as a congressman, worked as a banker, and President George Washington appointed him as the first Secretary of the Treasury. After the war Hamilton got into a fight with Aaron Burr over politics and was killed in a pistol duel. Hamilton's son was killed in a duel on the same site three years before his father.

Thaddeus Kosciuszko, a soldier of Polish-Lithuanian descent, traveled to America at the onset of the Revolution and volunteered for service. During the war, he served in the army as Washington's chief engineer and expert in the construction of field fortifications (then known as redoubts). Washington often misspelled the engineer's name, but highly valued his expertise. At the end of the war after seven long years of devoted service, Congress promoted Kosciuszko to the rank of brigadier general, gave him a generous land grant, and conferred upon him American citizenship. Kosciuszko, however, returned to Europe, where he continued his military service as the commander in chief of the Polish-Lithuanian Army in a war against Russia. Today, his name continues to be misspelled, but Thaddeous Kosciuszko is an honorary citizen of France, and a national hero in the United States, Belarus, Poland, and Lithuania.

Another Polish émigré volunteered for service in Washington's army in 1776, and is known today as the "father of the American cavalry." Casimir

Pulaski was already a hero of Poland when he joined the American "Continental Line" Army. Pulaski was a fierce warrior and a gallant cavalry leader who told General Washington, "I came here, where freedom is being defended, to serve it, and to live or die for it." Pulaski led numerous successful cavalry charges of both French and American soldiers until he was killed at the Battle of Savannah in October of 1779. Today, Pulaski Day is celebrated in several American states, and throughout the United States his name is honored with bridges, parks, streets, and even a ballistic missile submarine: the USS *Casimir Pulaski*.

Technically speaking, the final battle fought during the American Revolution occurred off the coast of India at the Cuddalore. There, a British fleet (18 warships) led by Admiral Sir Edward Hughes attacked a French fleet (15 warships) commanded by Bailli de Suffren. The battle was waged on June 20, 1783, before word had reached the combatants that the war was over. For three hours, the huge sailing ships belched fire from their cannons. Miraculously, neither side sustained major loss of life and not a single ship was sunk. Shortly after disengaging from battle, messages reached the combatants that the war was over.

*   *   *

What's in a Name?

Well, as it turns out, quite a bit. The famous Battle of Bunker Hill was fought on June 17, 1775, during the Siege of Boston. However, it was mostly fought on adjacent Breed's Hill. Bunker Hill was close by and peripherally involved, but the heaviest part of the battle was on property owned by the Breed family.

The mistake may rest with Abigail Adams, who watched the fighting from afar and wrote to her husband John about a friend who died "on Bunker Hill."

United States Armed Forces Commanders (1776-1783)

Department	Commander	Time Frame of Command
US Armed Forces	George Washington	Duration of war
Eastern Department	Artemas Ward	4 Apr 1776-20 Mar 1777
	William Heath	20 Mar 1777-7 Nov 1778
	Horatio Gates	7 Nov 1778-Nov 1779
Northern Department (New York Department)	Philip Schuyler	25 Jun 1775-19 Aug 1777
	Horatio Gates	19 Aug 1777-17 Apr 1778
	John Stark	17 Apr 1778-19 Oct 1778
	Edward Hand	19 Oct 1778-20 Nov 1778
	James Clinton	20 Nov 1778-25 Jun 1781
	John Stark	25 Jun 1781-15 Oct 1781
	William Alexander Stirling	15 Oct 1781-21 Nov 1781
	John Stark	21 Nov 1781-29 Aug 1782
	William Alexander Stirling	29 Aug 1782-15 Jan 1783
Southern Department	Charles Lee	1 Mar 1776-9 Sep 1776
	Robert Howe	9 Sep 1776-25 Sep 1778
	Benjamin Lincoln	25 Sep 1778-13 Jun 1780
	Horatio Gates	13 Jun 1780-31 Oct 1780
	Nathanael Greene	31 Oct 1780-end of war

United States Armed Forces Commanders (1776-1783) (continued)

Department	Commander	Time Frame of Command
Western Department	Edward Hand	10 Apr 1777-26 May 1778
	Lachlan McIntosh	26 May 1778-20 Feb 1779
	Daniel Brodhead	5 Mar 1779-24 Sep 1781
	William Irvine	24 Sep 1781-end of war
Highlands Department	William Heath	12 Nov 1776-21 Dec 1776
	Alexander McDougall	21 Dec 1776-12 May 1777
	Israel Putnam	12 May 1777-16 Mar 1778
	Alexander McDougall	16 Mar 1778-20 May 1778
	Horatio Gates	20 May 1778-24 Nov 1778
	Alexander McDougall	24 Nov 1778-27 Nov 1779
	William Heath	27 Nov 1779-21 Feb 1780
	Robert Howe	21 Feb 1780-21 Jun 1780
	Alexander McDougall	21 Jun 1780-3 Aug 1780
	Benedict Arnold	3 Aug 1780-25 Sep 1780
	George Washington	25 Sep 1780-28 Sep 1780
	Alexander McDougall	28 Sep 1780-5 Oct 1780
	Nathanael Greene	5 Oct 1780-17 Oct 1780
	William Heath	17 Oct 1780-11 May 1781
	John Paterson	11 May 1781-24 Jun 1781
	Alexander McDougall	24 Jun 1781-18 Jan 1782
	William Heath	18 Jan 1782-24 Aug 1782
	Henry Knox	24 Aug 1782-end of war

United States Armed Forces Commanders (1776-1783) (continued)

Canadian Department	Richard Montgomery	9 Dec 1775-31 Dec 1775
	David Wooster	31 Dec 1775-6 Mar 1776
	Charles Lee	17 Feb 1776-1 Mar 1776
	John Thomas	6 Mar 1776-1 Jun 1776
	John Sullivan	1 Jun 1776-2 Jul 1776
	Horatio Gates	17 Jun 1776-troops withdrawn from department

American (Continental) Soldiers During the American Revolution

The United States Army was officially formed by an act of Congress on June 14, 1775, from volunteer militiamen who initially served their respective colonies or states. Once independence was declared and the armed forces organized, the land component (known as the Continental Line or Army) was reorganized into departments, and the individual state regiments were incorporated under the command of General George Washington.

In 1789, Secretary of War Henry Knox reported the following as the number of soldiers (excluding militia) serving in the Continental Line Army:

1775	27,443
1776	46,891
1777	34,820
1778	32,899
1779	27,699
1780	21,015
1781	13,292
1782	14,256
1783	13,476

General Washington followed British doctrine and precedents in the establishment of the Army. He organized his roughly 27,000 men into six combat brigades of 2,400 men each, with supporting units to maintain them. The early fighting was largely contained in Massachusetts and New York, but the focus of the Revolution shifted south as the war progressed. While the Army evolved significantly during the war and its strength declined each year after 1776, General Washington maintained a constant presence in the

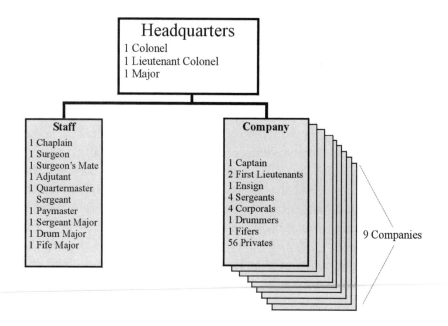

* This organization sets forth the authorized organization for a British Regiment. In practice, and especially as the war dragged on, the organization of regiments varied widely depending upon casualties, sickness, the ability to resupply and reorganize, and other factors.

American Infantry Regiment

field. More than any single person, it was his steady hand and clear strategic head that held the Army and the new country together long enough to defeat the largest and most powerful armed force of the 18th Century.

American regiments averaged 474 men, but this number declined from 1776 to 1783. The American armed forces also included Marines, a small navy, and individual militia units, but the bulk of the American armed forces during the Revolution resided in the Continental Army.

Most states during the American Revolution organized their military units by regional military districts, which raised individual companies and organized them into regiments. The Continental Congress ordered each state to follow strict guidelines in the way it raised and organized its units. However, differences in population, dialects, communications, war status, and a general reluctance to take commands from a superior Federal government (as opposed to a sovereign state) impeded the effort to create a smooth-functioning national Army. As a result, Congress allowed the inception of specialty units (such as rangers and partisan militias) in rural areas, and generally accepted whatever organizations the states managed to contribute to the war effort.

The bulk of the Army was comprised of infantry regiments, dragoons (light cavalry that frequently fought dismounted), and artillery. In an effort to better structure the military, in 1776 Congress reorganized the military areas of the armed forces into four separate territorial departments: Southern, Middle, Northern, and Canadian. In practice, military efforts shifted to meet enemy offensives, so the new departmental structure was largely organized only on paper. The war as experienced by the American Army was perhaps best described by General Nathanael Greene when he observed, "We fight, get beat, rise, and fight again." Fighting, losing, and fighting again hurts the morale and bleeds away the strength of any army, and so it was with the new American organization. After 1776, the numbers on the muster rolls declined and the Continental regiments underwent many transformations. As the units were reorganized, some regiments disappeared only to reappear with another numerical designation, usually combined from other units in the same situation. Consequently, some men fought in essentially the same regiment, but with a different numerical designation. However, most of these units remained assigned to their original state organizations within the Continental line.

Some of the units that fought for the American Army, and the battles in which they served, included:

1st Connecticut Regiment: September of 1776. Fought throughout the New York Campaign, Hudson Highlands, Philadelphia Campaign, Monmouth Court House, and was assigned to duties in New York.

The Delaware Regiment: December of 1775. Assigned to the defense of the Chesapeake Bay, fought throughout the New York Campaign, Trenton, Princeton, Monmouth Court House, and Greene's Southern Campaign. Reorganized in 1777, 1778, and 1780.

14th Massachusetts Regiment: April of 1775. Fought in the Siege of Boston, Canada, Lake Champlain, Trenton, Princeton, Saratoga, Philadelphia Campaign, Monmouth Court House, and Rhode Island.

Brewer's Regiment: April of 1775. This independently organized unit participated in the Siege of Boston. It was then reorganized and incorporated into the Continental Line in December of 1775.

1st Maryland Regiment: January of 1776. Assigned to the defense of the Chesapeake Bay, fought throughout the New York Campaign, Trenton, Princeton, Monmouth Court House, and Greene's Southern Campaign.

3d New York Regiment: October of 1775. New York Campaign, Saratoga, Philadelphia Campaign, Monmouth Court House, and the Iroquois Campaign (also known as Sullivan's Expedition).

8th Pennsylvania Regiment: January of 1776. New York Campaign, Trenton, Princeton, Philadelphia Campaign, and the Iroquois Campaign (also known as Sullivan's Expedition). Assigned to the defense of New Jersey and Pennsylvania.

3d Continental Light Dragoon Regiment (Baylor's and Lady Washington's Horse): January of 1777. The Philadelphia Campaign, Charleston, and Greene's Southern Campaign.

Continental Artillery Regiment (Gridley's and Knox's Artillery Regiment): May of 1775. Reorganized frequently during the war's early years until disbanded in January 1777. Saw action at the Siege of Boston, New York Campaign, Lake Champlain, Trenton, Princeton, and the Philadelphia Campaign. The bulk of the regiments (1st, 2nd, and 4th) were combined into a Continental Artillery Brigade led by Henry Knox, who rose to the rank of brigadier general before war's end. Knox capably commanded Washington's artillery during the Siege of Yorktown.

British and Hessian Commanders
(1775-1783)

Position/Department	Commander	Time Frame of Command
	Key British Administrative Leaders	
King: Great Britain (Captain General)	King George III	Duration of war
(1) Commander in Chief: British Armed Forces (General on the Staff)	Sir Jeffrey Amherst	1778-1782 (This post was vacant from 1775-1777)
(2) Commander in Chief: British Armed Forces (General on the Staff)	Sir Henry Seymour Conway	1782-1783
Prime Minister	Lord Frederick North	1775-1783
(1) Secretary at War	Lord Viscount George Barrington	1775-1779
(2) Secretary at War	Sir Charles Jenkinson	1779-1783
Secretary of State for the Colonies	Lord George Germain	1775-1783
	British Military Land Force Commanders in Chief (North America)	
(1) Commander in Chief (North America)	General Sir Thomas Gage	1763-Oct 10, 1775
(2) Commander in Chief (North America)	General Sir William Howe	Oct 10, 1775- May 20, 1778

British and Hessian Commanders
(1775-1783) (continued)

Position/Department	Commander	Time Frame of Command
(3) Commander in Chief (North America)	General Sir Henry Clinton	May 20, 1778-February 22, 1782
(4) Commander in Chief (North America)	General Sir Guy Carleton	February 22, 1782-November 28, 1783
	British Royal Navy Commanders	
First Lord of the Admiralty	John Montagu, 4th Earl of Sandwich	1775-1783
(1) Vice Admiral of the Blue-Royal Navy (North America) Commanded at the Siege of Boston.	Vice Admiral Samuel Graves	1776-1779
(2) Vice Admiral of the Blue-Royal Navy (North America) Commanded at the Siege of Charleston and the Battle of Cape Henry.	Vice Admiral Mariot Arbuthnot	1779-1781
(3) Vice Admiral of the Blue-Royal Navy (North America) Commanded at the Battle of the Chesapeake (loss led to surrender at Yorktown)	Vice Admiral Thomas Graves (nephew of Samuel Graves)	1781
(1) Commanded the Royal Navy Fleet (British West Indies)	Admiral John Byron	1778-1779

British and Hessian Commanders (1775-1783) (continued)

Position/Department	Commander	Time Frame of Command
(2) Commanded the Royal Navy Fleet (British West Indies). Commanded at Gibraltar and the Battle of the Saints.	Admiral George Rodney	1779-1781
	Major Northern Department Campaigns	
Massachusetts (Lexington, Concord, Siege of Boston) The war begins.	General Thomas Gage	1775-1776
New York (scored major victories driving Washington out of New York.)	General William Howe	1776-1777
Canadian and Saratoga (Surrendered his 5,800-man army at Saratoga—a major turning point in the war.)	General John Burgoyne	1777-1778
Hudson Highlands and Rhode Island (Battles fought in the Hudson Valley resulted in major losses for the British; they retreated to a stronghold in New York. Newport, Rhode Island is captured by the British.	General Henry Clinton	1777-1778
Philadelphia and New Jersey (Culminated with Battle of Monmouth, the last major pitched battle in the North.)	General William Howe	1777-1778

British and Hessian Commanders (1775-1783) (continued)

Position/Department	Commander	Time Frame of Command
	Major Southern Department Campaigns	
Carolinas (1st Battle of Charleston, Sullivan's Island)	General Henry Clinton & Commodore Peter Parker	1776
Savannah (Battles fought throughout Georgia and Florida.)	General Augustine Prevost	1778-1779
Carolinas, 2nd Battle of Charleston (Captured 5,283 American soldiers in the worst Patriot loss of the war.)	General Henry Clinton	1779
Carolinas, Virginia, or the Siege of Yorktown (Surrendered his army—7,087 men, effectively ending the war.)	Lord Earl Charles Cornwallis	January 1780-October 1781
	Florida (West) Territory	
Siege of Pensacola (Lost Florida to Spain and surrendered 2,200 men to General Gálvez.)	General John Campbell	March 9-May 8, 1781
	Mississippi Territory	
Battles of Mobile, Nachez, and Manchac (Lost Mississippi to Spain and surrendered 1,000 men to General Gálvez.)	General John Campbell	1780-1781

British and Hessian Commanders (1775-1783) (continued)

Position/Department	Commander	Time Frame of Command
	Canadian Department	
(1) Canadian Department (Governor) Commanded at battles of Quebec, Valcour Island, Lake Champlain, Hudson Valley Campaign.	Major General Sir Guy Carleton	1775-1778
(2) Canadian Department (Governor) Commanded Tory and Indian raids of the Mohawk Valley, and defense of Canada.	Major General Sir Frederick Haldimand	1778-1783
	Hessian (German Allied Troops)	
(1) Commander in Chief	Lieutenant General Leopold Phillip von Heister	1776-1778
(2) Commander in Chief	Lieutenant General Baron Wilhem von Knyphausen	1778-1782
(3) Commander in Chief	Lieutenant General Friedrich Wilhem von Lossberg	1782-1783
(4) Commander in Chief	Lieutenant General Wilhem August Donop	1782-1783
Commander of German and Indian Troops (Canadian and Saratoga Campaigns)	Major General Friedrich Adolf Riedesel	1776-1777

British and Hessian Commanders (1775-1783) (continued)

Position/Department	Commander	Time Frame of Command
German Regimental & Division Commanders	Major General Johann Stirn	1778-1779
	Major General von Mirbach	1778
	Major General Schmidt	1778-1779
	Major General Baron von Lossberg	1778-1781
	Major General von Bose	1778-1781
	Major General von Huyne	1778-1780
	Major General Heinrich von Kosporth	1779-1783
	Major General Friedrich von Hackenberg	1780-1783
	Major General Uphraim von Gosen	1781-1783
	Major General Hans von Knoblach	1781-1783
	Major General Carl Ernst von Bischausen	1781-1783
	Major General Friedrich von Wurmb	1782-1783
	Major General Johan von Loos	1783

British Soldiers in the American Revolution

During the 18th Century, the army of Great Britain served as the "backbone" of the Crown. As the executor of the King's will, these soldiers were professionally trained and thoroughly proficient in their duties. The regiments of foot (or infantry) bore the burden of war and served as the primary military resource on America's battlefields. The infantry were usually supported by light cavalry or dragoons and artillery, but the foot soldier's primary purpose was to close with and destroy his enemy. Marching directly into battle and fighting in tight linear formations required tremendous discipline and confidence in one's officers and comrades. England's army excelled in all these categories and was (and still is) universally recognized as the finest military machine of its age.

When the American Revolution erupted in 1775, England had 70 regiments of foot. During the course of the war that number was expanded to 105 regiments. Each regiment was comprised of eight battalion companies. These companies were supported by one light company and one grenadier company. These were employed on the regiment's flanks or wherever the commander maneuvered them to protect his main force or deploy rapidly for offensive operations. Each regiment was organized with 811 officers and men under the command of a colonel. The commander had 40 officers, 72 non-commissioned officers (NCOs), 24 drummers, two fifers, and 672 privates. Each regiment carried three non-existent men on the rolls to provide adequate pay to maintain uniforms and for whatever else the commander chose to do with the funds to maintain his unit.

The British infantryman carried the .75 caliber flintlock musket known affectionately as the "Brown Bess." This 15-pound weapon was used with great effect in massed formations and was tipped with a foot-long bayonet, which the soldiers were famous for wielding in battle. The grenadier company was comprised of the largest and strongest men available to the commander. These men typically wore tall bearskin hats and were considered an elite outfit and the most intimidating soldiers on the battlefield. The light infantry was a mobile reserve of maneuverable physically adept men who were normally used as rangers. In addition to their muskets, they were often armed with hatchets and knives, and so were outstanding in close-quarter fighting.

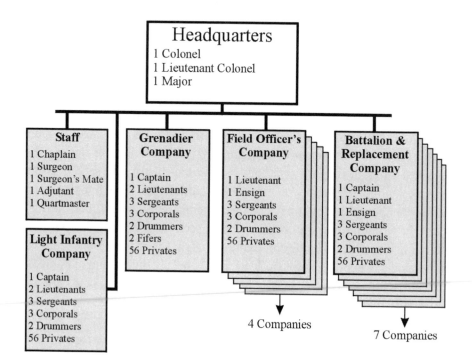

* This organization sets forth the authorized organization for a British Regiment. In practice, and especially as the war dragged on, the organization of regiments varied widely depending upon casualties, sickness, the ability to resupply and reorganize, and other factors.

British Infantry Regiment

England was stretched to the breaking point during the American Revolution. In addition to maintaining units at home for defensive purposes, England employed land and naval assets across much of the globe, from the West Indies to the East Indies.

Some of the units that fought for the British Army, and the battles in which they served, included:

1st Regiment of Foot Guards: Arrived in America in 1776 (New York). Fought at Long Island, Fort Washington, Philadelphia Campaign, Brandywine, Monmouth Court House, Charleston, Guilford's Courthouse, Green Spring, and surrendered at Yorktown, Virginia.

21st Regiment of Foot (Royal North British Fusiliers): Arrived in Quebec in 1776. Fought at Lake Champlain and Burgoyne's Campaign (captured at Saratoga).

46th (Cornwall) Regiment of Foot: Arrived in America in 1776 (North Carolina). Fought at Charleston. Transferred north and fought in the New York Campaign, Philadelphia Campaign, Brandywine, and Monmouth Court House. Reorganized and transferred to the West Indies in 1777.

71st Regiment of Foot (Fraser's Highlanders): Arrived in America in 1776 (New York). Fought at Long Island, Fort Washington, Forts Clinton and Montgomery, Philadelphia Campaign, and Stony Point. Sent to Savannah in 1778 and fought at Briar Creek, Stono Ferry, Augusta, Savannah, Charleston, Camden, Cowpens, Guilford Courthouse, Green Spring, and Yorktown (captured).

55th (Westmoreland) Regiment of Foot: Arrived in America in 1775 (Boston). Fought at the Siege of Boston, New York Campaign, Philadelphia Campaign, and Monmouth Court House. Transferred to East Florida and St. Kitts in 1779.

17th Regiment of Light Dragoons: Arrived in America in 1775 (Boston). Fought in the New York Campaign, Long Island, Fort Washington, Princeton, Forts Clinton and Montgomery, Philadelphia Campaign, Whitemarsh, and Monmouth Court House. Elements transferred to Charleston in 1779 as the British Legion (led by Lt. Col. Banastre Tarleton), and fought at Blackstock's Plantation, Cowpens, Guilford Courthouse, and Yorktown (captured).

British (Provincial American) Loyalists in the American Revolution

During the American Revolution, at least 25,000 men sided with England and fought as Tories or Loyalists. Several thousand Loyalists also joined the English Navy and served as sailors or even privateers. These men fought and died alongside their British counterparts in nearly every battle of the long and bloody war. Loyalist units with enough men to form companies, battalions, and regiments were organized and equipped just like regular British regiments.

In addition to their services to the Crown, many of these men fought as partisans, especially in the Southern states. The majority of the combatants who fought in the bloody battles waged in the backwoods of the Carolinas, Georgia, and Florida were Americans—either Tory or Patriot. For example, Major Patrick Ferguson commanded the British Provincial Militia (Ferguson's Corps) during the fighting in South Carolina and served as its brigadier general in the debacle at Kings Mountain, where all of the combatants (with the exception of Ferguson) were Americans.

The Loyalists provided invaluable service to the Crown in both numbers and intelligence. They knew the terrain better than their English counterparts and their supporting network of informants provided excellent information on enemy activity. Loyalist service to the Crown divided families and communities, and often led to acts of vengeance and retribution. After the war, many Loyalists moved abroad to avoid retribution for having supported England during the war.

Some of the Loyalist or Tory units that fought for the British, and the battles in which they served, included:

American Legion: 1780: 400 men. Raised in New York and fought at Portsmouth and New London.

American Volunteers: 1779: 1,000 men. Raised in New York and South Carolina by Lt. Col. Patrick Ferguson. Fought at Savannah and Kings Mountain, where the entire unit was captured or killed.

Duke of Cumberland's Regiment: 1781: 600 men. Raised in Charleston from Continentals captured at the Battle of Camden. Deployed to Jamaica in 1781.

East Florida Rangers (Kings Rangers): 1779: 860 men. Raised in Georgia and Florida by Lt. Col. Thomas Brown. Fought at Savannah and Augusta. Merged with the Georgia Loyalists in 1782.

Jamaica Legion and Jamaica Volunteers: 1779: 600 men. Raised in Jamaica by British Governor John Dalling. Participated in raids in Nicaragua and Honduras.

King's American Regiment: 1776: 833 men. Organized by Colonel Edmund Fanning in New York and fought at Forts Clinton and Montgomery, Charleston, and Savannah. Elements also served in East Florida, Kings Mountain (captured), and in Georgia.

Maryland Loyalists: 1777: 425 men. Raised by Lt. Colonel James Chalmers in Maryland and Pennsylvania. Served in New York and Halifax until transferred to Pensacola, where they surrendered in 1782.

Philadelphia Light Dragoons: 1777: 120 men. Raised by Captain Richard Hoveden and was used to augment the British Legion and the King's American Dragoons in battle at Savannah, Charleston, Cowpens, Guilford Courthouse, and Yorktown (captured).

Royal Ethiopian Regiment: 1775 (Virginia): 300 men. Organized by Virginia's Royal Governor John Murray (Lord Dunmore). This unit was comprised of blacks who were promised freedom in return for their services to the Crown. Fought at Norfolk and Great Bridge, Virginia.

Volunteers of Ireland: 1777: 871 men. Raised in Pennsylvania and served in the New York Campaign, Charleston, Camden, and Hobkirk's Hill. Assigned to the British Army as the 105th Regiment of Foot in 1782.

West Jersey Volunteers: 1778: 200 men. Raised in Philadelphia and served in the New York Campaign. Merged into the New Jersey Volunteers.

French Soldiers in the American Revolution

In June of 1776, France began to secretly provide financial assistance to the rebellious English colonists in America. The French were less concerned with the concept of liberty than causing problems for England, their longtime enemy. When it seemed as if the Americans had a chance to actually defeat the British (the victory at Saratoga in late 1777 was the tipping point), France embraced the fledgling democracy with a formal alliance signed in Paris on February 6, 1778. The French formally recognized American independence on May 4, 1778. France viewed its participation in the war as a way to enlarge its empire at England's expense. Thousands of troops and tons of materiel were poured into the colonies and elsewhere to fight England. French officers (most notably Marquis de Marie Jean Paul Joseph Roche Yves Gilbert du Motier Lafayette) volunteered to serve in the American army at their own expense. Congress eventually appointed the capable Lafayette to the rank of major general, and he led American troops in the Continental Army.

In the summer of 1778, French Admiral Charles Hector T. d'Estaing sailed his fleet up the North American coast, confronted a British fleet under Admiral William Howe at Newport, Rhode Island, and engaged in important operations off New York. The French Navy carried the war to the British across the globe, threatening their far-flung possessions and forcing England to commit precious resources at many other points other than America. In 1779, Admiral d'Estaing assisted the Americans by attacking British land forces at Savannah, Georgia (September 23 – October 20). From February through May 1780, the French allies assisted the Americans during their unsuccessful defense of Charleston, South Carolina.

Setbacks during the early joint French-American operations notwithstanding, in July of 1780 Jean Baptiste Donatien de Vimeur, Comte de Rochambeau arrived at Newport, Rhode Island, with an entire corps. A French fleet under Francois Joseph Paul, Comte de Grasse-Tilly inflicted a decisive strategic defeat against Admiral Thomas Graves's British warships at the Battle of the Capes (September 5-8, 1781). The victory isolated Lieutenant General Charles Cornwallis and his army on the Yorktown peninsula in Virginia. Six thousand French soldiers joined with their American allies there in a campaign that led to Cornwallis's surrender on

October 5, 1781. Without the assistance of the French during the American Revolution, the war may not have ended in an American victory.

The 23 infantry regiments and detachments of engineers, miners, artillerymen, and dragoons committed by France to assist the Americans during the Revolutionary War were arranged in two separate corps. The first French ground campaign deployed to America in September of 1779. These 4,000 soldiers were commanded by Admiral d'Estaing and Count Arthur Dillon. The second major deployment was in July 1780, when Comte de Rochambeau arrived at Newport, Rhode Island, with about 6,000 men. Additional French troops were delivered by Admiral de Grasse, who sailed his fleet from the West Indies to participate in the Yorktown Campaign in August 1781. The ground troops were led by Major General Marquis Claude Henri de Rouvroy, Comte de Saint-Simon.

Some of the units that fought for the French, and the battles in which they served, included:

Agénois Infantry regiment: (Savannah: *d'Estaing,* Yorktown: *Saint-Simon*, Pensacola)

Hainault Infantry regiment: (Savannah: *d'Estaing*)

La Sarre Infantry regiment: (Yorktown: *Rochambeau*)

Soissonnais Infantry regiment: (Rhode Island, Yorktown: *Rochambeau*)

1st Legion Marine Volunteers: (Yorktown: *Saint-Simon*)

2nd Legion of Lauzon Volunteers: (Yorktown: *Rochambeau*)

Spanish Soldiers in the American Revolution

The 16th, 17th, and 18th centuries witnessed the dominant powers in Europe struggling for control of land and resources across much of the Western hemisphere, and especially in North America. Spain had colonies in southern North America and maintained outposts in Florida and Louisiana, as well as in the southwestern United States (then wilderness territories) in California, Arizona, New Mexico, and Texas. It also controlled strategic points along the Mississippi River. Spain also had colonies in Cuba, Puerto Rico, Hispaniola (Dominican Republic and Haiti), and Central America (then called Nueva Espana or "New Spain"). After the voyages of Cortez and others, Spain conquered and controlled virtually all of South America.

When hostilities erupted in the American colonies in 1775, Spain had already been at war with England for many years. With the Treaty of 1763, which marked the end of the Seven Years' War (known in America as the French and Indian War), Spain officially ceded Florida to England, even though Spanish settlers in sizeable numbers remained there. Spain managed to wrest "Louisiana" from France, but British opportunists worked against Spanish interests by allying themselves with the Indians who lived throughout that expansive region.

In 1776, the Spanish provided financial and materiel support to the American colonists. Like France, Spain looked for any opening to weaken and harass its enemy. Spanish support became more tangible in 1778 and 1779 when large quantities of gunpowder, arms, and ammunition arrived to directly support General George Rogers Clark in his victories against the British at Kaskaskia, Cahokia, and Vincennes. The Spanish also assisted the Americans in the destruction of British outposts along the Mississippi River. Spain formally allied itself with America and France by declaring war against Great Britain on June 21, 1779. Spain and England engaged in a variety of conflicts across the globe, with King Carlos III encouraging his armed forces to fight the British wherever they could, and to exploit opportunities in the wild regions of North America.

During this time the Spaniards continued expanding their influence and settlements in western North America, knowing England had an interest in the same region. When English explorers patrolled the northwest Pacific, coast Spain dispatched soldiers to "Alta California" to defend it from enemy incursions. Spanish outposts were constructed at Ventura, Los Angeles, Santa Barbara, San Diego, Monterey, and San Francisco. Settlements were also expanded along the Colorado River, where Yuma Indians fought with the Spanish settlers. British invasions of Nicaragua and Honduras triggered other fighting, as did sea battles in the Caribbean and off Gibraltar. All of this took place during our own American Revolution.

All of this took place between 1775-1783, but Louisiana and Florida were the primary battlegrounds between Spain and England most associated with the American Revolution. The war forced England to reinforce possessions in West Florida at Pensacola and in East Florida at St. Augustine. Attacks by American expeditionary forces from Georgia against the latter outpost failed to throw out the British. In 1779, the Spanish ruler of Louisiana, Governor General Bernardo Gálvez, organized, equipped, and prepared an invasion force to attack the British stationed in West Florida and throughout the Mississippi basin.

General de Gálvez marched his command from New Orleans north to Manchac, Louisiana, where he attacked the British at Fort Bute and forced its surrender on September 7, 1779. He also attacked and captured British outposts at Baton Rouge, Louisiana and Natchez, Mississippi, later that month. Following up on these successes, Gálvez marched into West Florida and laid siege to the British fort at Mobile (now Alabama) from January 28 to March 9, 1780. The king of Spain provided financial support for the American Revolution (several hundred million in today's dollars) and Gálvez personally collected donations from the citizens of Cuba, which were also handed over to the Americans. Additional Spanish involvement included a combined operation against West Florida at Pensacola.

Once General Galvez's armada secured the Mississippi region and defeated the British in West Florida, the French contingent sailed to the West Indies, where it rendezvoused with Admiral de Grasse's French fleet. Gálvez, meanwhile, obtained additional funding to pay for French operations in America. While he secured both Spanish and French interests from British attack in West Florida and in the West Indies, the French fleet sailed north for Virginia, where it defeated the British fleet in the Battle of the Capes, trapped Lord Cornwallis at Yorktown, and assisted in the siege that essentially ended England's commitment to defeat the American rebellion.

Some of the Spanish units that fought during the American Revolution included:

Battalion of Negroes of Havana (Cuba)
Cavalry Regiment Lusitania
Fixed Infantry Regiment of Louisiana
Havana Fijo (Fixed) Regiment (Cuba)
Infantry regiment of Betschart
Infantry regiment de Hibernia
Infantry regiment of Guadalajara "El Tigre" (Mexico)
Infantry regiment of Milicias Pardos de Merida y Yucatan (New Spain)
Infantry regiment of Naples (Spain)
Infantry regiment of Puerto Rico (de la Raza)
Light Dragoons of New Spain
Line Cavalry of the King Foot
Line Cavalry of the Prince
Louisiana Infantry Regiment
Louisiana Dragoon Company
Militia of the German Coast (Louisiana)
Militia (Mississippi River Volunteers)
Militia of New Orleans (Battalion of Disciplined Militia-Louisiana)
Militia of New Orleans (Distinguished Company of Carabiniers-Louisiana)
Royal Corps of Artillery
Royal Artillery of Louisiana
Spanish Frontier Dragoons

Hessian Soldiers in the American Revolution

Germany was not yet a nation when the first muskets were discharged on Lexington Green in 1775, but soldiers from independent German states were hired by England to augment its army during the American Revolution. By the time the Treaty of Paris was signed in 1783, nearly 29,000 Germans had served under the Union Jack. These troops hailed from six German states: Hesse-Cassel, Hesse Hanau, Brunswick, Waldeck, Anspach-Beyreuth, and Anhalt Zerbst. The Crown contracted directly with individual German princes for these men, a common protocol during the eighteenth century. The primary core of German (or Hessian) soldiers were provided by Friedrich II, the Landgraf (German noble) of Hesse-Cassel. Friedrich II committed fifteen "Regiments of Foot" (infantry) as well as support troops and resources to assist Great Britain with the rebellion in its American colonies. The professionally trained German soldiers served valiantly and suffered at least 2,300 casualties during the war.

Each Hesse-Cassel regiment was comprised of five companies with a paper total of 650 men. Each of these regiments was reduced by one grenadier company that was used to form four grenadier battalions comprised of 524 men each. An additional Jager Corps (also known as chasseurs, which translates to "huntsmen") was organized to provide the Hessians with an elite unit of hand-selected warriors. These men were among the tallest and strongest soldiers. The Jagers fielded 600-700 men during the war and achieved notable battlefield success. Three companies of artillery supported the Hesse Cassel regiments. Thus, the primary Hessian force deployed to fight in America was composed of fifteen infantry regiments, four grenadier battalions, one Jager Corps, and three artillery companies. The Hesse Cassel troops were divided into two divisions. Lt. General Leopold von Heister commanded the First Division, and Lt. General Wilhelm von Knyphausen commanded the Second Division. The Hesse Cassel units that fought in America arrived in two expeditionary forces at New York in August of 1776.

Troops from the German state of Brunswick formed the second largest Hessian force—five infantry regiments, one grenadier battalion, one regiment of dragoons, a Jager Corps, and a support artillery unit. The Brunswick troops were initially sent into Quebec in June of 1776. These men served the British throughout the war in Canada and participated in Burgoyne's disastrous New York campaign.

Anspach-Beyreuth provided two infantry regiments, one Jager Corps, and miscellaneous supporting units. The German states of Hesse Hanau, Waldeck, and Anhalt Zerbst each provided one infantry regiment and their own supporting artillery. All of these units participated in combat with the exception of the Anhalt Zerbst units, which did not arrive in Quebec until May of 1778. However, they were stationed in New York from 1781-1783.

Hessian organizations were associated with unique names as opposed to numerical designations. Many units adopted the name of their commander ("Chef"), who was usually a colonel. However, some units were named in honor of fallen commanders or someone else chosen for the honor. The various regiments and the major battles in which they participated are listed below. (1st Div. or 2nd Div. indicates the division to which Hesse Cassel units were assigned.)

Some of the Hessian units that fought for the British, and the battles in which they served, included:

Hesse Cassel: (12,805 troops)
Field Jager Corps: (This unit or detachments thereof fought in every Hesse Cassel operation.)
Fusilier Regiment von Ditforth: (1st Div., Fort Washington, White Plains, Newport, Charleston.)
Fusilier Regiment Erbprinz: (1st Div., Long Island, Fort Washington, Yorktown.)
Fusilier Regiment von Knyphausen: (1st Div., Long Island, White Plains, Fort Washington, Trenton (captured; reorganized elements fought at Brandywine.)
Fusilier Regiment von Lossburg: (1st Div., Long Island, Fort Washington, White Plains, Fort Washington, Trenton (captured; reorganized elements fought at Brandywine.)
Grenadier Regiment von Rall: (1st Div., Long Island, White Plains, Fort Washington, Trenton, Brandywine, East Florida, Savannah, Charleston.)
Regiment of Dragoons Prinze Ludwig: (Bennington, Saratoga)
Regiment von Specht: (Saratoga)
Hesse Hanau: (2,038 troops) Arrived at Quebec in June of 1776.

The Dutch in the American Revolution

The involvement of the Dutch Republic (more commonly known as the Netherlands, or officially as the Republic of the Seven United Netherlands) in our American Revolution is a classic example of the war's global ramifications. The country was led during the revolution (1776-1783) by Prince William V. Although he was a cousin of King George III of England, William did not agree with how the English treated the American colonies.

Political scrabbles between the royal hierarchies and interrelated oligarchies resulted in entangling yet fragile alliances. The Dutch people cared little about what happened in America, but the war offered the ruling elite and merchants opportunities to provide assistance to the colonists and reap profits in return. The burgeoning colonial commerce in the Caribbean was of particular interest to the Dutch, who maintained a sovereign commercial hub on their island of St. Eustatius (known as "Statia"), which would ultimately play a key role in the American Revolution.

As early as 1756, "Statia" operated a free and independent port. Because it was a neutral port, the British could not restrict trade there or impose maritime actions against shipping that utilized Statia. During the early 1770s, the Americans found a convenient and supportive trade route through which they could ship war materiel to feed their revolution against Great Britain. Untaxed indigo, rice, and tobacco passed through Statia for trade with Europeans. These items were exchanged for cannons, rifles, gunpowder, sugar, tea, and other staples for the return trip to the colonies.

After the colonists declared independence from England, the American brig *Andrew Doria* received the Navy's first official salute from a foreign nation at Statia on November 16, 1776. The act carried with it global significance because it made it easier for other European nations to also recognize the United States. Within a few years, France and Spain declared war against Great Britain and officially allied themselves with America.

Meanwhile, in 1779, Commodore John Paul Jones carried the war to the British when he brazenly attacked enemy warships in the waters off the home islands. When Jones set forth on his expedition, Benjamin Franklin encouraged him (if he was victorious) to sail on to the Netherlands. After his warship *Bonhomme Richard* defeated *HMS Serapis* in battle, Jones sailed his prize to the port in Texel, where he was praised by the Dutch for his courage.

The overtly political display earned Jones enduring fame and won much-needed Dutch support for the struggling American cause.

In 1780, HMS *Vestal* intercepted a ship carrying American diplomat Congressman Henry Laurens. Found among his belongings were documents that implicated the Dutch and their direct aid in the American cause. Great Britain threw Laurens into prison in the Tower of London and declared war on the Dutch on December 20, 1780, in what is known to the Europeans as the 4th Anglo-Dutch War (1780-1784).

Wasting no time, Admiral Sir George Rodney led the Royal Navy in an attack against the Dutch port of St. Eustatius. Among his prizes captured were 50 American warships and at least 2,000 American seamen. Additionally, the English captured 80 Dutch vessels, valuable cargoes, and a substantial amount of capital. In addition to the value of the port itself, the English gained valuable intelligence regarding the European trading firms associating themselves with the American cause.

In early August of 1781, Dutch and British fleets under Rear Admiral Johan Zoutman and Vice Admiral Sir Hyde Parker, respectively, met off the east coast of England in the North Sea at Dogger Bank. The British fleet comprised seven ships of the line: *Berwick* (74 guns), *Bienfaisant* (64 guns), *Buffalo* (60 guns), *Dolphin* (44 guns), *Fortitude* (74 guns—Parker's flag ship), *Princess Amelia* (80 guns), and *Preston* (50 guns). The Dutch (Netherlands) fleet also comprised seven ships of the line: *Admiraal de Ruijter* (68 guns—flag ship), *Admiraal Generaal* (74 guns), *Admiraal Piet Hein* (56 guns), *Argo* (40 guns), *Batavier* (50 guns), *Erfprins* (54 guns), and *Holland* (68 guns).

The bloody duel—the British suffered 400 casualties and the Dutch 500—ended in a tactical draw, although the Dutch declared the engagement a victory. However, the Dutch ships returned to port and did not leave to engage the British again, which left England in command of the North Sea. Despite the Dutch losses at Statia and Dogger Bank, American diplomats such as John Adams succeeded in persuading the Dutch to extend substantial loans to the United States, which greatly aided the fledgling republic.

In January of 1783, the Dutch participated in the ceasefire between Great Britain, France, the United States, and Spain. However, they refused to sign the Treaty of Paris that year, waiting until May of 1784 before officially agreeing to end hostilities with Great Britain.

Revolutionary War Battles, Chronological by State

Date	Battle	Campaign	State/Other
1783, April 17	Arkansas Post (Colvert's Raid)	Mississippi	Arkansas
1775, September 4-November 2	Fort St. John, Siege of	New York	Canada
1775, September 24-25	Montreal	Canada	Canada
1775, December 31	Québec	Canada	Canada
1776, March 3	Nassau	Caribbean	Caribbean (British Territory)
1778, February-April 1782	Caribbean	Naval Campaign-Caribbean	Caribbean (British Territory)
1781, September 6	New London (Fort Griswold and Groton Heights)	Arnold's Expedition	Connecticut
1778, December 29	Savannah	Southern	Georgia
1779, February 14	Kettle Creek	Southern	Georgia
1779, March 3	Brier Creek	Southern	Georgia
1779, September 16-October 19	Savannah, Siege of	Southern	Georgia
1780, September 14-18	Augusta	Southern	Georgia
1781, May 22-June 18	Augusta, Siege of	Southern	Georgia
1777, April-June 1780	British Isles	American Naval Campaign-Europe	Great Britain
1779, February 23-25	Fort Sackville	Illinois	Illinois

	Revolutionary War Battles, Chronological by State (continued)		
Date	**Battle**	**Campaign**	**State/Other**
1782, August 19	Blue Licks	Kentucky	Kentucky
1779, June 17-August 13	Penobscot Bay	Penobscot Expedition	Maine
1775, April 19	Lexington and Concord	Massachusetts	Massachusetts
1775, April 19-March 17, 1776	Boston, Siege of	Massachusetts	Massachusetts
1775, May 27-28	Hog and Noodle Islands	Massachusetts	Massachusetts
1775, June 17	Bunker Hill	Massachusetts	Massachusetts
1776, December 26	Trenton	New Jersey	New Jersey
1777, January 3	Princeton	New Jersey	New Jersey
1777, October-December	Forts Mercer and Mifflin, (Siege of Philadelphia)	Philadelphia	New Jersey
1778, June 28	Monmouth Court House	New Jersey	New Jersey
1775, May 10	Fort Ticonderoga	New York	New York
1776, August 27	Long Island	New York	New York
1776, September-November	New York (British Siege of Kip's Bay, Harlem Heights, Ft. Washington)	New York	New York
1776, October 11-13	Lake Champlain (Valcour Island)	New York	New York
1776, October 28	White Plains	New York	New York
1777, June 30-July 7	Fort Ticonderoga (Second battle of) and Hubbardton	Saratoga	New York
1777, August 6	Fort Stanwix and Oriskany	Saratoga	New York

Date	Battle	Campaign	State/Other
Revolutionary War Battles, Chronological by State (continued)			
1777, September 19	Freeman's Farm	Saratoga	New York
1777, October 7	Bemis Heights (Second Battle of Freeman's Farm)	Saratoga	New York
1779, July 16	Stony Point	New York	New York
1779, August 29	Newtown	Sullivan's	New York
1777, October 6	The Hudson Highlands (Battles of Fort Montgomery and Fort Clinton)	Saratoga	New York
1776, February 27	Moore's Creek Bridge	Southern	North Carolina
1781, February 25	Haw River (Pyle's Defeat and Pyle's Hacking Match)	Southern	North Carolina
1781, March 15	Guilford Court House	Southern	North Carolina
1781, April 25	Hobkirk's Hill	Southern	North Carolina
1777, September 11	Brandywine Creek	Philadelphia	Pennsylvania
1777, September 16	"The Clouds"	Philadelphia	Pennsylvania
1777, September 21	Paoli (Massacre of Paoli)	Philadelphia	Pennsylvania
1777, October 4	Germantown	Philadelphia	Pennsylvania
1777, December 5-7	Whitemarsh (Edge Hill)	Philadelphia	Pennsylvania
1778, July 3	Wyoming (Massacre of Wyoming)	Sullivan's	Pennsylvania
1778, August 29	Rhode Island	Rhode Island	Rhode Island
1775, October-December	Snow Campaign (Ninety-Six and Great Cane Brake)	Snow	South Carolina

\	**Revolutionary War Battles, Chronological by State** (continued)		
Date	**Battle**	**Campaign**	**State/Other**
1776, June 28	Fort Sullivan (First Battle of Charleston)	Southern	South Carolina
1779, June 20	Stono Ferry	Southern	South Carolina
1780, April 18-May 12	Charleston, Siege of	Southern	South Carolina
1780, October 7	King's Mountain	Southern	South Carolina
1780, November 20	Blackstock's Plantation	Southern	South Carolina
1781, January 17	Cowpens	Southern	South Carolina
1781, May 22-June 19	Ninety-Six, Siege of	Southern	South Carolina
1781, September 8	Eutaw Springs	Southern	South Carolina
1780, May 29	Waxhaws	Southern	South Carolina
1780, July 12	Williamson's Plantation (Huck's Defeat)	Southern	South Carolina
1780, August 6	Hanging Rock	Southern	South Carolina
1780, August 16	Camden	Southern	South Carolina
1780, August 18	Musgrove's Mill	Southern	South Carolina
1777, August 16	Bennington	Saratoga	Vermont
1775, December 9	Great Bridge	Virginia	Virginia
1781, July 6	Green Spring	Virginia	Virginia
1781, September 5-8	The Capes (French and British naval battle)	Yorktown	Virginia
1781, September 28-October 18	Yorktown, Siege of	Yorktown	Virginia
1776, July 1-December 1782	Cherokee Campaign (Second Cherokee War)	Cherokee	Virginia, Tennessee, North Carolina, South Carolina, Georgia, and Kentucky

MAPS

The pages that follow include a wide variety of theater, campaign, and tactical maps that depict both the expansive nature and reach of the American Revolution, as well as some of its most important campaigns and battles at the tactical level.

Few people realize that the fighting in the Revolution was as far west as the Mississippi River, as far south as the Gulf of Mexico, and that sea battles directly affecting the outcome of the were fought hundreds and in some cases, thousands of miles away from the American Colonies.

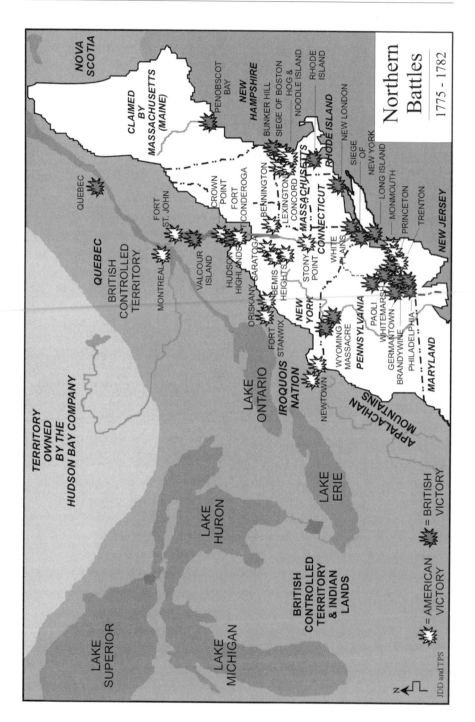

Northern Battles
1775 - 1782

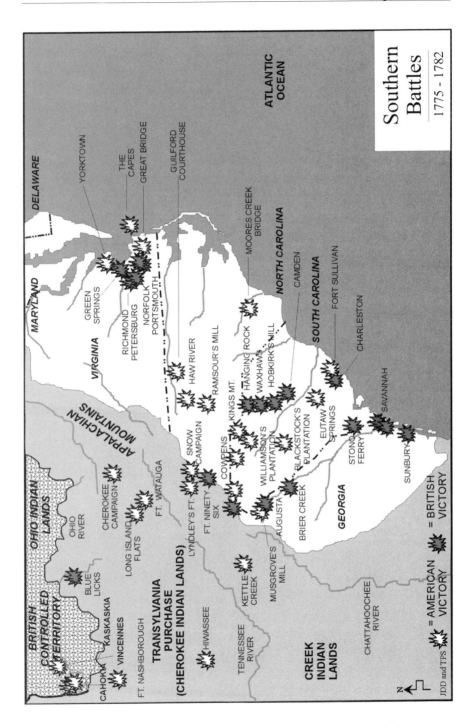

Southern Battles
1775 - 1782

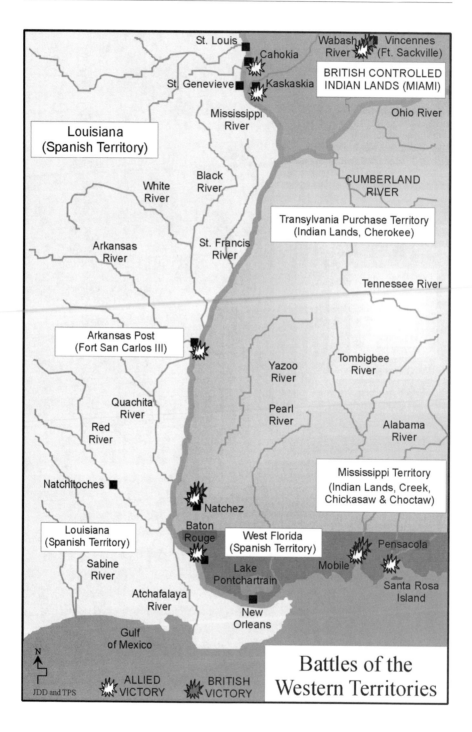

Battles of the Western Territories

Select Battles & Campaigns

Lexington and Concord, Battles of (Boston Campaign)

Date: April 19, 1775

Region: Northern Colonies, Massachusetts

Commanders: British: Lieutenant Colonel Frances Smith, Major John Pitcairn, Major (Lord) Hugh Percy; American: Captain John Parker (Lexington), Colonel James Barrett (Concord and along British retreat to Charlestown-Boston)

Time of Day / Length of Action: Early morning (Lexington and Concord), morning and afternoon (retreat to Boston)

Weather Conditions: Unremarkable, clear and pleasant

Opposing Forces: British: 700-man force of infantry, grenadiers, Royal marines with cavalry escort (reinforced with 1,000 soldiers and two cannons during retreat phase); American: 70 at Lexington; 200 at Concord, with more along British retreat to Charlestown (loosely organized local militia units).

British Perspective: By the spring of 1775, the American colonies were on the verge of revolt. Nowhere was this radical energy more fervent than in Boston and the surrounding countryside, where British troops eyed the locals with justifiable suspicion. In the port of Boston, British authorities focused closely on the export businesses as local merchants sought ways around the numerous tariffs imposed by the Crown. Smuggling was rampant. New Englanders avoided high taxes by trading illegally with the Dutch and French. Violent protests in the streets of Boston reached a new phase on March 5, 1770, when British troops fired into a mob killing five protestors. Anti-British sentiment escalated over the next few years.

In May of 1774, Lt. Gen. Thomas Gage, the commander-in-chief of the British Army in America, returned to the colonies after a leave in England and assumed command as the military Royal Governor of Massachusetts. Rebellion loomed as the Crown implemented additional retaliatory measures for what it deemed rebellious acts against the King's authority.

The colonials established a Massachusetts Provincial Congress in May 1774, which met illegally in Concord. Its leadership included John Hancock and Samuel Adams. In February of 1775, Parliament declared the colony of Massachusetts to be in open rebellion and authorized British troops to kill violent rebels. General Gage was ordered to quell the rebellious behavior. He was instructed to arrest the membership of the Massachusetts Provincial Congress, but decided instead to seize arms and munitions stored at Concord. During the early hours of April 19, he dispatched troops under Lt. Colonel Frances Smith and Maj. James Pitcairn to seize these munitions.

American Perspective: Burdensome taxes imposed by the Crown were enacted to recoup expenditures of the French and Indian War, but the American colonists despised the British authorities for their heavy-handed tactics. Between 1763 and 1765, the Americans were hit with the Sugar Act, Currency Act, and Quartering Acts. In 1767, the Massachusetts House of Representatives officially denounced a new tax known as the Townshend Act. Hailing these acts passed in England as "taxation without representation," disgruntled colonials subject to the Crown expressed their displeasure loudly and frequently. Royal Governor Sir Francis Bernard sought assistance from British authorities and on October 1, 1768, Boston was occupied by British soldiers. Parliament eventually repealed the Townshend Act, but its tax remained on imported tea. In 1773, the East India Trading Company enjoyed British favor as the primary importer of colonial tea, and an official decree known as the Tea Act was established to enforce it as policy. The colonists consumed tea with a passion, and the increased prices served only to further anger them.

On December 16, 1773, colonists covertly boarded an East Indian merchant ship laden with tea and poured it into the harbor. The consequence of what came to be known as "The Boston Tea Party" was the passage of a new imposition known as the Intolerable Acts, which included the closure of the port of Boston until restitution for the lost tea was made to the Crown. Previously elected officials were replaced with appointed British authorities, and private homes were seized to quarter British troops.

The establishment of the Massachusetts Provincial Congress in May 1774, coupled with the increased rhetoric against the Crown's authority, left the region a dry tinderbox awaiting a spark that arrived in the form of British troops marching from Boston to Concord.

Despite British efforts to march in secret to Concord, a network of local spies sounded the alarm. Two Bostonians, Paul Revere and William Dawes, avoided capture and slipped out of the city into the countryside. Before his departure Revere placed lanterns in the Old North Church to signal movement details of his enemy (which resulted in the well-known mantra "One if by land or two if by sea"). Dawes and Revere traversed different routes to warn colonials in Lexington that the British were on the march toward Concord. In Lexington, which lay on the road to Concord, another colonist named Samuel Prescott joined the "midnight riders" in order to spread the word to the rebels. British cavalry patrols captured Revere and forced Dawes away from the area, but Prescott reached Concord.

Shortly after Revere was captured the rebels assembled on Lexington Green. Led by their militia commander Capt. John Parker, the "Minutemen" waited for the main body of British troops marching rapidly toward Concord. The British would have to march through Lexington to reach their destination. The first clash of what would be a long hard war awaited them there. As the British approached the rebel position and the sunlight rose in the eastern sky, a scout returned with word the enemy had arrived.

Terrain: Gently rolling fertile farm region. Lexington and Concord are both small New England towns. In Lexington, the brief fight occurred on the town green. The Concord action began at the Concord North Bridge and continued along the retreat route to Charlestown, a dirt road lined with alternating forests and fields that provided the colonial militia with advantageous areas for picking off the retreating British soldiers.

The Fighting: (Battle of Lexington): Captain Parker organized his men on the town green to interrupt the march of the approaching British. The sun was just rising. The handful of rebels quickly realized they were heavily outnumbered and that defeat was inevitable. Captain Parker ordered his men to disperse. Exactly what took place next is not clear. As the British soldiers reached the green, someone may have fired into the British forces from behind a stone wall. Other shots rang out. Under Major Pitcairn's direction, the British returned fire and assaulted the colonials. The skirmish ended quickly with the blood of eighteen rebels spilled onto Lexington Green (eight killed, ten wounded).

Battle of Concord: The British resumed their march to Concord, six miles distant. News the British were coming had reached Concord about 2:00 a.m., and several companies of minutemen turned out. Local militia leader Col. James Barrett led a contingent of men to remove munitions and military stores from his property and conceal them elsewhere. Others watched for the enemy from a ridge lining the road leading to town. They fell back when the Redcoats approached Concord between 7:00 and 8:00 a.m. Captain Lawrence Parsons led three companies to search homes and farms to

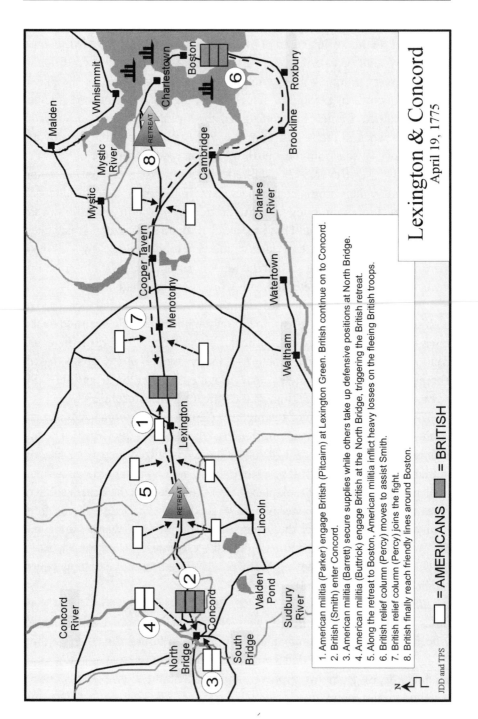

Lexington & Concord
April 19, 1775

1. American militia (Parker) engage British (Pitcairn) at Lexington Green. British continue on to Concord.
2. British (Smith) enter Concord.
3. American militia (Barrett) secure supplies while others take up defensive positions at North Bridge.
4. American militia (Buttrick) engage British at the North Bridge, triggering the British retreat.
5. Along the retreat to Boston, American militia inflict heavy losses on the fleeing British troops.
6. British relief column (Percy) moves to assist Smith.
7. British relief column (Percy) joins the fight.
8. British finally reach friendly lines around Boston.

☐ = AMERICANS   ▨ = BRITISH

JDD and TPS

uncover the hidden weapons and powder while three other companies under Capt. Walter Laurie secured the North Bridge. The British set fire to several cannon mounts in the courthouse. The colonials watched in horror, certain the enemy was torching the town.

By this time (perhaps 9:30 a.m.), 300 to 400 militia had gathered on the high ground above the North Bridge. With fife and drum Maj. John Buttrick led his motley group of farmers and merchants toward Laurie's companies defending the span. Laurie ordered his men to fall back to the opposite side of the bridge, where they deployed in a tight in-depth defensive formation that allowed only one of the three companies to fire on the approaching rebels, who continued advancing unaware of the brief fight at Lexington. When the British opened fire the rebels confidently returned it. The exchange lasted for several minutes and eventually drove the Crown's professional soldiers back in some disorder into Concord. They left three killed and eight wounded on the field. The Americans, who suffered two killed and three wounded, made no real attempt to pursue Laurie or cut off the column of British out searching Barrett's farm. A chagrined Lieutenant Colonel Smith led his men out of Concord about noon, cognizant that the force of Massachusetts militiamen was growing.

Retreat to Charlestown: The British passed through a hail of enemy lead as they withdrew from Concord to Lexington. Just outside Lexington, Captain Parker, who had earlier led the militia on Lexington Green, organized an ambush known today as "Parker's Revenge." Parker's surprise attack inflicted many casualties and wounded key British leaders, including Lt. Col. Francis Smith. A British relief force led by Maj. (Lord) Percy joined Smith's column at Lexington. Without Percy's men, artillery, and leadership, the colonials may have overwhelmed and destroyed Smith's expeditionary force. Using his cannon to disperse the advancing rebels, Percy regained some control of a difficult withdrawal. Although Percy managed to lead the British column back to the safety of Charlestown, the rebels fired on it from the woods throughout much of the march, inflicting several hundred casualties. By the time the march ended, some 6,000 colonial militiamen had assembled on the outskirts of Boston.

Casualties: British: 73 killed, 174 wounded, and 26 missing; American: 49 killed, 41 wounded, and five missing (most losses on both sides incurred during the running battle to Charlestown).

Outcome / Impact: The Battles of Lexington and Concord ("The Shot Heard Round The World") initiated armed hostilities between the British and American forces. The bloodshed was exactly what many in the colonies were hoping for to raise popular support for an armed revolution. The colonial fighting style was unconventional and disorganized, but the asymmetric form of warfare had a tremendous impact upon the morale of the British soldiers, who suffered nearly 20 percent casualties. The seemingly invincible British army suddenly found itself in a war fighting an enemy who used tactics as foreign to them as the soil upon which they were fighting. Colonial Gen. William Heath organized the thousands of militiamen milling about outside Boston and established a quasi "siege" around Gage's shocked British command. The war was now on in earnest.

Today: The Minute Man National Historical Park in Concord interprets and preserves these opening battles of the war through exhibits and living history programs.

Further Reading: Tourtellot, Arthur Bernon, *Lexington and Concord: The Beginning of the War of the American Revolution* (Norton, 2000); Forthingham, Richard, *History of the Siege of Boston and the Battles of Lexington, Concord, and Bunker Hill; Also, An Account of the Bunker Hill Monument with Illustrative Documents* (Scholars, 2005); Hibbert, Christopher, *Redcoats and Rebels: The American Revolution Through British Eyes* (Norton, 2000).

Fort Ticonderoga, Battle of (Canadian Campaign)

Date: May 10, 1775
Region: Northern Colonies, New York
Commanders: British: Captain De La Place; American: Colonel Ethan Allen and Captain Benedict Arnold
Time of Day / Length of Action: Dawn
Weather Conditions: Unremarkable, spring morning
Opposing Forces: British: 85; American: 100 Vermont militiamen
British Perspective: Hostilities in Massachusetts were far removed from the stone ramparts of Fort Ticonderoga. Although the revolution had been underway for several weeks, most of the British outposts and garrisons in North America, including Ticonderoga, remained undermanned and isolated. As with any frontier outpost, the drudgery of daily routine and

isolation dulled the senses and lulled inhabitants into a false sense of security. Fort Ticonderoga was built by the French in 1755. By 1775 the post was armed with 79 pieces of heavy artillery, but had a garrison of only 85 soldiers. British authorities, however, believed it was adequately defended. There was no indication local citizens were preparing for an assault on the fort or that any hostile force was approaching.

American Perspective: Following the Battles of Lexington and Concord, the Second Continental Congress called up a national standing army, naming George Washington as its commander. Washington opened a quasi-siege against the British in Boston, Massachusetts. He and his officers realized from the outset they were short on nearly everything an army required, especially artillery and ammunition. The British outpost at Fort Ticonderoga 200 miles to the north had both guns and powder in substantial quantities. If the fort could be taken, its resources and strategic location would meet other needs as well. Colonel Ethan Allen organized a 100-man force of Vermont militiamen (known as the Green Mountain Boys) to conduct the difficult mission. Joined by Connecticut militia leader Captain Benedict Arnold, the Patriot force launched its effort to capture the British fort.

Terrain: Located in Essex County, New York, 95 miles north of Albany, Ticonderoga derived its name from the Indian word *Cheonderoga*, or "Place between two waters." Fort Ticonderoga was strategically located on dominating high ground surrounding the area between Lake Champlain and Lake George in the Hudson River Valley.

The Fighting: Before dawn on May 10, the Green Mountain Boys stealthily crossed Lake Champlain from Vermont into New York. The Vermonters crept undetected up to the fort's stone walls. To their surprise, the raiders discovered an unmanned and unlocked entrance, through which they quietly entered the bastion. As they hoped, except for a single guard the garrison was sound asleep. A brief fight broke out during which the lone British guard and a Vermonter were wounded. The Americans moved quickly to the commander's quarters, where Captain De La Place awoke slowly to the realization that his fortress had been captured by the enemy. When Colonel Allen demanded his surrender, the sleepy De La Place, who was still in his bedclothes, asked, "To whom and why?" Colonel Allen recalled in his memoirs that he replied in a firm, loud voice, "In the name of the Great Jehovah and the Continental Congress!" The startled British commander ordered his men to stand down and surrendered the fort.

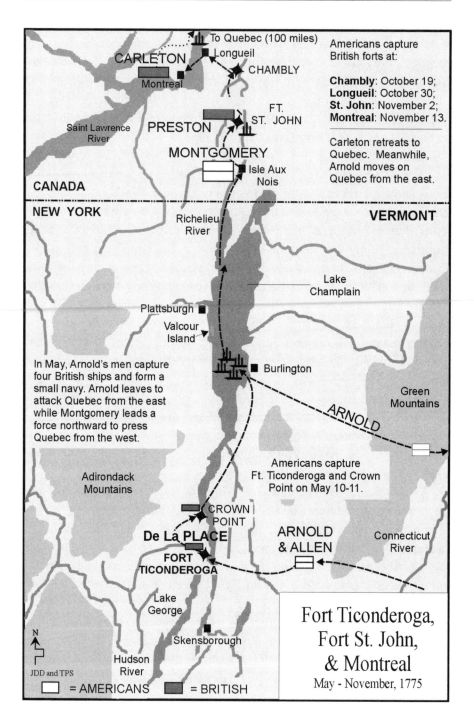

Americans capture
British forts at:

Chambly: October 19;
Longueil: October 30;
St. John: November 2;
Montreal: November 13.

Carleton retreats to
Quebec. Meanwhile,
Arnold moves on
Quebec from the east.

To Quebec (100 miles)

CARLETON

Longueil

CHAMBLY

Montreal

Saint Lawrence
River

PRESTON

FT.
ST. JOHN

MONTGOMERY

Isle Aux
Nois

CANADA

NEW YORK

Richelieu
River

VERMONT

Lake
Champlain

Plattsburgh

Valcour
Island

In May, Arnold's men capture
four British ships and form a
small navy. Arnold leaves to
attack Quebec from the east
while Montgomery leads a
force northward to press
Quebec from the west.

Burlington

Green
Mountains

ARNOLD

Adirondack
Mountains

Americans capture
Ft. Ticonderoga and Crown
Point on May 10-11.

De La PLACE

CROWN
POINT

ARNOLD
& ALLEN

Connecticut
River

FORT
TICONDEROGA

Lake
George

N

Skensborough

Hudson
River

JDD and TPS

☐ = AMERICANS   ☐ = BRITISH

**Fort Ticonderoga,
Fort St. John,
& Montreal**

May - November, 1775

Casualties: British: one wounded; American: one wounded.

Outcome / Impact: In addition to the vast supply of munitions and 79 artillery pieces that went with the capture of Fort Ticonderoga, the fledgling Patriot army achieved a magnificent public relations victory. The artillery that could be moved was hauled overland to Boston and emplaced in the siege works. Fort Ticonderoga became an important base for the Americans. Had it remained in British hands, it would have posed a dangerous threat to operations in the Hudson River Valley. On May 11 (the day after Ticonderoga fell), the Vermont raiders also captured the British fort at Crown Point several miles north of Ticonderoga. The embarrassment of these twin military failures humiliated the British while offering an invaluable morale boost for the nascent Continental army and the Patriot movement throughout the colonies.

Today: Fort Ticonderoga National Historic Landmark hosts nearly 100,000 visitors each year and includes a wide variety of living history programs and interpretive events. Fort Crown Point in New York preserves and interprets American, British, and French history.

Further Reading: Hamilton, Edward Pierce. *Fort Ticonderoga: Key to a Continent* (Ft. Ticonderoga, 1995); Pell, Stephan H. P. *Fort Ticonderoga: A Short History Compiled from Contemporary Sources* (n.p., 1957).

Long Island, Battle of (New York Campaign)

Date: August 27-29, 1776

Region: Northern Colonies, New York

Commanders: British: General Lord William Howe, Lieutenant Generals Henry Clinton, Charles Cornwallis, and Lieutenant General Leopold Philip von Heister; American: General George Washington, Major General Israel Putnam, Brigadier Generals John Sullivan and William (Lord Stirling) Alexander

Time of Day / Length of Action: 3:00 a.m to 2:00 p.m.

Weather Conditions: Unseasonably cool summer weather with heavy rain and fog

Opposing Forces: British Army: 24,600 plus 5,000 Hessians; British Navy: 10,000; American Army: 19,000

British Perspective: After evacuating Boston, the British reorganized and focused their efforts on New York. On June 25, 1776, Gen. William Howe, who replaced Thomas Gage as the Crown's commander-in-chief in the colonies, led an armada to Sandy Hook, New Jersey, which guarded the southern entrance to New York harbor. From that station the Royal Navy could guard the harbor entrance while the army disembarked to prepare for land operations. On July 12, Admiral Richard Howe joined his brother William and delivered to him additional troops and 150 more ships. Augmenting these forces was Maj. Gen. Sir Henry Clinton and his armada, fresh from the ill-fated attempt to take Charleston (Fort Sullivan, June 28, 1776). With a combined arms task force of nearly 40,000 men and several hundred warships, the Crown was finally well prepared to stamp out the war wrought by her rebellious colonies.

From local Loyalists British intelligence learned the rebels were deployed in defensive positions along Brooklyn (Guian) Heights, where they had prepared a series of forts and interconnecting trenches to protect New York City from invasion. Spies also provided the British with information about weaknesses in the lines that offered tempting targets. Howe promptly made plans to exploit them. Mindful of the stiff resolve the Americans had demonstrated in Massachusetts, Howe planned his offensive operations in New York with more deliberation and care.

Early on the morning of August 22, Howe led the first batch of 20,000 men in an amphibious assault against Long Island. The initial part of Howe's force (about 4,000 men) launched from Staten Island and landed on the southwest side of Long Island near New Utrecht. The rest of the army followed while powerful naval warships provided cover. None was needed. By noon, more than 15,000 men and dozens of artillery pieces had been put ashore. A march four miles inland to Flatbush resulted in a sharp skirmish on August 23 with advance elements of the Patriot command on Long Island. On August 25, more British landed southeast of Denyse's Point, augmenting Howe's effective force to more than 20,000 men. He split his army into two roughly 10,000-man wings. By the morning of August 27 he was in position to begin his offensive.

American Perspective: Having successfully defended Massachusetts, General Washington anticipated the British would move to New York. He established a defensive network around that city's harbor, a vast undertaking for a fledgling army supported by only a tiny and untried navy. Still, recruits flooded to the cause and by August of 1776 the nascent colonial army filled fortifications and defensive positions around the city with 19,000 troops.

The terrain on Long Island was similar to that of Boston and its harbor, though much larger in area. For Washington and the Patriots, the devil was in the vexing details: how to defend a vast area against overwhelming land and naval forces. Washington's men were predominantly inexperienced and inadequately trained and equipped for the task Washington set for them, which was to hold both New York City and Brooklyn (on Long Island), or at least extract precious blood and treasure from the Crown before giving them up. The architect of Long Island's defense was Nathanael Greene, a capable field commander who had a decent grasp of the terrain and the men assigned to defend it.

Greene concentrated his resources in a line anchored by three small forts named Putnam, Greene, and Box along Guian Heights (also called Brooklyn Heights). The line was reinforced by felled trees and good fields of fire. It offered a three-mile barrier along a natural neck of strategic terrain that would have to be taken if New York was to be threatened by a ground assault. Other forts positioned along the harbor shore defended against any maritime assault directed at New York. As the Americans were about to learn, however, things could go very wrong in a hurry.

Two days before the British began landing operations against the southwest coast of Long Island Greene fell sick with a fever and was replaced by John Sullivan. The change erased Greene's extensive knowledge of the terrain and disposition of the defenders from the battle about to unfold. Four days later Sullivan was superseded by Maj. Gen. Israel Putnam. Putnam was a hard fighter, a trait amply demonstrated at Boston, but most observers agree he was not capable of managing the large scale field action presented by the Long Island campaign; he knew even less about Long Island's terrain than Sullivan.

Howe began landing troops on August 22. Washington was in New York City. Though he shuttled over reinforcements, he was unsure whether Howe's Long Island effort was his primary attack or merely a large diversion. Within less than one week (August 20-26), however, Howe had landed a mammoth army and marched several miles inland, seriously threatening the Guian ridge. By the time sunset arrived on August 26, Washington knew the hammer was about to fall on Long Island.

Israel Putnam, who had no idea where the British would attack his front, was tasked with overseeing essentially two defensive lines perpendicular to one another. Exactly how many Americans were deployed on Long Island is open to some speculation. The main line held approximately 6,500 men deployed around Brooklyn and faced generally southeast. This line ran north for one and one-half miles from the mill dam–Gowanus Creek area that emptied into Gowanus Bay to Wallabout Bay. The remaining 3,000 soldiers were deployed to guard four strategic natural passes cut by major roads leading to the top and beyond the heights. About 550 men were on the far left guarding Gowanus Road overlooking the bay of the same name. About one and one-half miles east were 1,100 men guarding Flatbush Pass. One mile farther east, 800 soldiers blocked Bedford Pass. Still farther east on the far left flank of Putnam's attenuated line were another 500 riflemen. They were tasked with picketing a thin line stretching toward Howard's Tavern at Jamaica Pass—Putnam's extreme (and very vulnerable) left flank.

Terrain: New York City occupied the land on Manhattan Island, where the Hudson, Harlem, and East rivers converge to empty into New York harbor. Long Island (now part of New York City) measures 118 miles long (roughly north to south) and 20 miles at its widest point (roughly east to west). There was only one connector to the mainland of New York, which was on the north side of Manhattan at Kingsbridge on the Harlem River. In 1776, Long Island was a mixture of heavily forested hills and pastoral rolling farmland that included several small towns such as Flatbush, Bedford, and Brooklyn.

The battle took place in the northwestern section of the island on Guan (or more popularly Brooklyn) Heights. This high ground ran generally west to east. It was anchored on the west above Gowanus Bay and ran east by northeast several miles into Long Island. The heights were more abrupt on their southern (British) side, towering at some points 80 feet above the lower approaching elevations. The result was an imposing natural barricade to General Howe's advance. The high ridge was cut by four major roads, which dictated to a large degree where the Patriot defenders deployed.

The Fighting: General Howe's plan was simple. A strong 5,000-man column under Gen. James Grant would move against Putnam's far right flank above Gowanus Bay to divert Patriot attention to the western end of the line. In conjunction with Grant, a Hessian column of similar strength under von Heister would move against and hold in place the enemy center around Flatbush. While the enemy focused attention on their center-right, Howe (with Generals Cornwallis and Clinton) would march east and then north with 10,000 men beyond and behind Putnam's left flank, rolling up and crushing the Patriot army strung out along the high ridge.

The battle opened just after midnight on the morning of August 27, when General Grant moved his 5,000 British soldiers north along the Gowanus Road and began skirmishing with rebel defenders. Putnam was advised about 3:00 a.m. of the enemy move and ordered Gen. William (Lord Stirling) Alexander to advance to the far right with reinforcements. He did so and deployed about 1,600 men to confront his much stronger opponent. Grant stopped his column in front of the rebel line and shelled the Patriots, threatening them with an infantry attack. General Sullivan, meanwhile, had reached the center of the line near Flatbush Pass, where he discovered von Heister's Hessians menacing his front with artillery—but nothing more. Playing into Howe's hands, Sullivan dispatched troops west to reinforce Alexander. By 8:00 a.m. Washington arrived on Long Island.

When the firing began early on the Patriot right and center, Col. Samuel Miles moved his Pennsylvania riflemen west toward the combat, leaving Jamaica Pass (Putnam's extreme left flank) unguarded. Ordered to return to the pass, Miles arrived just in time to spot the tail end of Howe's column (his baggage train) rolling through the defile. Miles realized the peril of the unfolding situation and sent about half his men toward the main line to warn their comrades and escape the closing trap. With his remaining men (about 250) he attacked the baggage train. It was a forlorn hope, though a brave effort. In addition to killed and wounded, 160 of the riflemen were captured, including Miles. Howe's plan was working perfectly.

The large British turning column marched completely behind Putnam's line and reached Bedford about 8:30 a.m. Thirty minutes later (after Miles's attack) Howe fired a pair of signal guns to alert Grant and von Heister to attack the front of the heights while Howe advanced against the rear. However, only the Germans attacked. Von Heister's advance north up the main road in the center of the battlefield struck General Sullivan's defenders, who faced pressure from both front and rear. Within minutes the Patriot line unraveled east to west (left to right) as men dashed along the wooded heights in an effort to reach the safety of the main Brooklyn line. Sullivan and many of his men were captured near Baker's Tavern, where a stout but short defense was attempted. Pressed by the Hessians in front and Howe's column behind them, the defenders had nowhere to run and surrendered or were shot down.

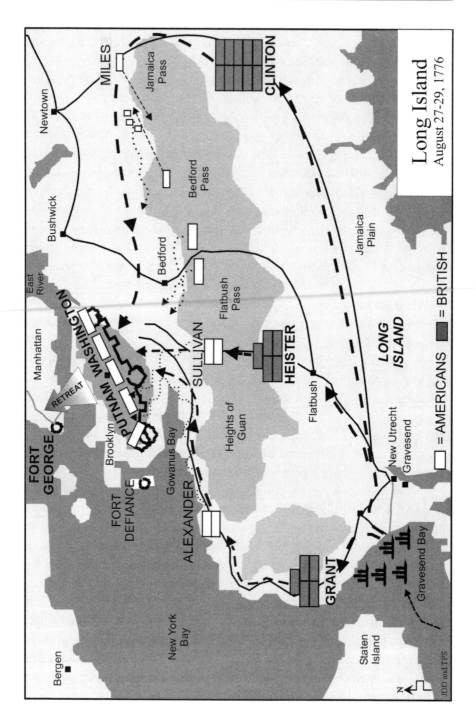

Long Island
August 27-29, 1776

By 11:30 a.m., Alexander's infantry holding Putnam's far right flank above Gowanus Bay were overwhelmed by Grant's numerically superior command, which finally moved forward in a decisive attack that broke apart the Patriot line. Most of the fleeting Americans headed for Gowanus Creek in an effort to escape the closing enemy jaws. When Cornwallis and the 71st Regiment of Highlanders were discovered blocking their route of retreat, Alexander launched a series of daring counterattacks with about 250 Maryland riflemen led by Maj. Mordecai Gist. The bold tactical effort allowed some of his men to escape across Mill Dam Road, but Alexander was unable to clear a path of retreat for the bulk of his command. Most of the attackers, including Alexander, were captured.

After soundly sweeping Putnam's defenders off the Guian high ground, Howe interrupted his own brilliantly conceived and executed battle plan. Hours of daylight were still left to him, but instead of regrouping and attacking the last line of Patriot defense, he halted his army, reorganized his command, and ordered entrenchments dug facing the Patriot defensive works. With control of the East River, Howe apparently believed Washington was trapped and at his mercy. The two armies remained in place as rain curtailed aggression throughout the next day. Luckily for the Patriots, heavy winds prevented Howe's warships from moving behind Washington's trapped army. On the evening of August 29, Washington ordered boats to be gathered to withdraw his troops from Brooklyn Heights. A heavy fog, rain, and wind helped mask his narrow escape. By the next morning the Americans were safely across the river. That same day, Howe's warships moved up the river, a few hours too late to effectively end the American Revolution in 1776.

Casualties: British: 63 killed, 314 wounded; American: Estimates vary widely, from 800 (Washington) to 6,000 (Clinton). A reasonable tabulation is 300 killed, 650 wounded, and 1,100 captured (2,050 all causes).

Outcome / Impact: The fight on Long Island was a terrible defeat for the colonial army. The loss of Greene to fever and the consequent elevation of Putnam to command weakened what was otherwise a reasonably sound defensive deployment. The failure to properly guard the far left allowed a 10,000-man column to slip around unnoticed, ensuring defeat. The failure to effectively use cavalry to watch the flank was inexcusable. The resounding military defeat sent morale plummeting and caused many to question Washington's fitness for high command. The British war machine—large, well supplied, and supported by the world's most powerful navy—seemed unstoppable. Howe's star was ascendant (though his hesitation after his initial victory let Washington slip from his grasp). Only weeks earlier, the colonists had declared to the world their intent to break away by signing the Declaration of Independence. After Long Island, the freedom-seeking Americans were not as confident of final victory.

Further Reading: Bliven, Bruce, Jr. *Under the Guns: New York: 1775-1776* (Harper & Row, 1972); Gallagher, John J. *The Battle of Brooklyn, 1776* (Da Capo, 2001).

Hubbardton, Battle of (Saratoga Campaign)

Date: July 7, 1777

Region: Northern Colonies (New York and Vermont)

Commanders: British: Major General John Burgoyne, Major General Friedrich von Riedesel, and Brigadier General Simon Fraser; American: Lieutenant Colonel Seth Warner

Time of Day / Length of Action: Early morning, three hours

Weather Conditions: Clear and warm

Opposing Forces: Totals: British: 1,030 (advance guard); American: 1,100 (rear guard)

British Perspective: In the spring of 1777, Maj. Gen. John Burgoyne was dispatched to Québec to take charge of British forces in Canada and lead an offensive into western New York, where he was to crush Patriot forces in that region. He would then march south to Albany and join forces with Gen. William Howe's army for additional offensive operations. Burgoyne left 3,700 troops in Canada with Gen. Sir Guy Carleton while he led a 9,100-man expeditionary force south along Lake Champlain to capture Fort Ticonderoga. At the same time, another British force, about 2,000 men led by Lt. Col. Barry St. Leger, would march around to the west and attack Patriots operating in the Mohawk Valley before moving to Albany. Howe, meanwhile, would lead the main British army north up the Hudson River from New York City to join St. Leger and Burgoyne at Albany. If successful, the three-pronged offensive would crush the rebellion in New York and separate New England from the rest of the colonies. It was an ambitious plan, but if successful offered perhaps the best way to cripple the rebellion and turn the tide of the war decisively in the Crown's favor.

Burgoyne reached Fort Ticonderoga in late June, and after initial delay captured critical high ground that made the occupation of the fort untenable. General Arthur St. Clair evacuated Fort Ticonderoga on the night of July 5. When Burgoyne discovered the withdrawal the next morning, he ordered a vigorous pursuit to catch and destroy the Patriot army. Brigadier General Simon Fraser's British and Maj. Gen. Friedrich von Riedesel's Hessians joined forces on the afternoon of July 6 and camped later that day just three miles from the American rear guard. When the enemy was discovered so close, Fraser determined to attack them in the morning.

American Perspective: General Burgoyne's invasion from Canada forced the scattered Patriots to funnel south to Fort Ticonderoga, where they joined with men led by Maj. Gen. Philip Schuyler, the commander of American troops in western New York (Northern Department of the Continental Army). One of his subordinates, Gen. Arthur St. Clair, was assigned to defend Fort Ticonderoga and the surrounding region. When Burgoyne arrived and secured high ground southwest of the fort on Mt. Defiance, St. Clair ordered his men to evacuate (some by water, others by land) after dark on July 5. Colonel Pierce Long, tasked with covering the main withdrawal route of American forces, was nearly trapped in Skenesboro on the afternoon of July 6, but he set fire to the town and slipped off in the confusion toward Hubbardton (now East Hubbardton), Vermont.

St. Clair, meanwhile, led the largest contingent of his army, about 2,500 men, overland south through Castleton with the intention of joining up with Colonel Long and much of the army's artillery train at Skenesboro. On the way they passed through the tiny village of Hubbardton. Militia officer Seth Warner was left behind on a piece of high ground to guide trailing regiments on to Castleton. Instead of the 150 men St. Clair intended, Warner ended up with about 1,000 soldiers in a camp around which he failed to post pickets.

Terrain: Warner's troops occupied a 1,000-foot elevation east of what is today known as East Hubbardton. This hill is the dominant terrain feature in an area known for its thickly wooded hills.

The Fighting: Warner's men held an advantageous position (known today as Monument Hill), but without a proper advance guard the position was nearly worthless against a determined and veteran enemy. Fraser attacked with 750 men from the west at 4:40 a.m. The initial wave struck a regiment of New Hampshire troops commanded by Col. Nathan Hale (not the better-known Hale) while they were cooking breakfast along a small stream. The assault routed the New England infantry. Warner and another regimental commander, Col. Turbott Francis, hastily formed their regiments and unleashed a volley into the front line of attackers, killing and wounding two dozen including some high ranking field officers. The fighting front stabilized into a 900-yard line stretching from 1,200-foot rocky and wooded Zion Hill on the American left into the woods on the far right. Forced to advance under fire uphill, the redcoats had a harder time of it.

A good tactician, Fraser quickly realized the hill was the key terrain on the field and stripped his own left flank to increase the punch on his right. Either forced back or by design, the American left flank on the hill slowly bent backward, which made it harder for the British to find the flank and turn and collapse it. Colonel Francis commanded on the American right and gained ground there with his Massachusetts infantry against the weakened British left flank. All along the line the Patriot infantry enjoyed the advantage of fighting Indian-style from behind trees and rocks—tactics the British did not fully understand or train for. The fighting was at close quarters and the result was mounting British losses.

Fortunately for Fraser, von Riedesel arrived with his grenadiers and jägers. He, too, was a capable officer and quickly realized the difficulties they were facing that morning. Without wasting time, the German general pitched in his troops as quickly as they arrived, some directly forward and others around to find and roll up the American flank. Von Riedesel ordered his band to play and his men to sing, which had a tendency to unnerve enemy troops and convince them they were facing overwhelming numbers. Within a few minutes Colonel Francis was shot dead (after the battle von Riedesel saw to it he received a Christian burial), the grenadiers had found Francis's flank, and the Massachusetts regiment was falling back. When Fraser's men finally launched a bayonet attack against the Vermont troops on the high ground, Warner knew he had pushed his luck as far as possible. Instead of ordering a traditional withdrawal, he spread the word to "scatter and meet me back at Manchester." Most of Warner's men managed to reassemble and continue evading the enemy southward to Bennington, Vermont.

The heavy battle had seesawed back and forth in the Vermont thickets for more than two hours. One of the war's leading historians claims the forgotten battle of Hubbardton was "as bloody as Waterloo" when one considers the proportion of casualties to the numbers involved (roughly one in four of those involved in the fighting was either killed, wounded, or captured). However, estimates of the losses on both sides vary considerably.

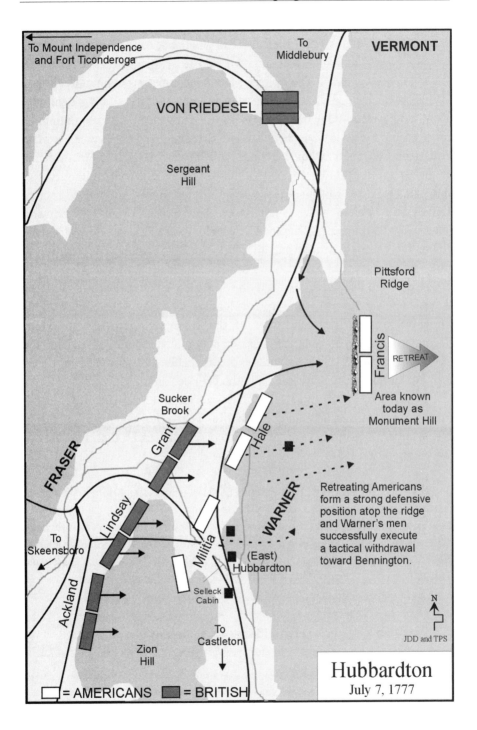

To Mount Independence
and Fort Ticonderoga

To
Middlebury

VERMONT

VON RIEDESEL

Sergeant
Hill

Pittsford
Ridge

Francis

RETREAT

Area known
today as
Monument Hill

Sucker
Brook

Grant

Hale

FRASER

Lindsay

WARNER

Retreating Americans
form a strong defensive
position atop the ridge
and Warner's men
successfully execute
a tactical withdrawal
toward Bennington.

To
Skeensboro

Militia

(East)
Hubbardton

Ackland

Selleck
Cabin

N

To
Castleton

To
Castleton

Zion
Hill

JDD and TPS

☐ = AMERICANS   ▨ = BRITISH

Hubbardton

July 7, 1777

Casualties: British: 35 killed and 150 wounded; American: 40 killed, 40 wounded, and 234 captured (estimates), and 12 artillery pieces lost.

Outcome / Impact: The delaying action combat at Hubbardton was a British tactical success but an American strategic victory. Warner's initially inept stand succeeded in delaying Burgoyne's advance long enough to put a more comfortable distance between the British army and St. Clair's main American column. St. Clair marched southward in Vermont to Fort Ann and farther south to Fort Edward on the Hudson River. His route to the frontier outposts along the Hudson River wound through a thickly forested region, throughout which the Patriots felled trees from Skenesboro to Fort Edward. They also dug ditches and emplaced obstacles at strategic locations along the route, all of which slowed pursuit. The British eventually covered the 20 miles, but it took them three weeks to perform the arduous task. On July 29 Burgoyne and his army reached the outskirts of Fort Edward, but the Americans were by this time in the vicinity of Sarotoga. In hindsight, we know today that the evacuation of the American garrison from Fort Ticonderoga, coupled with the delaying action at Hubbardton, signaled the beginning of the end of Burgoyne's campaign. He would surrender his entire army to Horatio Gates just three months later at Saratoga.

Today: The Hubbardton Battlefield is a Vermont State Historic Site that hosts an annual reenactment of the battle. The visitor center offers period artifacts, a fiber-optic map of the engagement, and other interpretive information.

Further Reading: Cook, Fred J. *Dawn Over Saratoga: The Turning Point of the Revolutionary War*. Garden City, NY: Doubleday, 1973; Ellis, Davis M. *The Saratoga Campaign*. New York: McGraw, 1969; Luzader, John: *Saratoga: A Military History of the Decisive Campaign of the American Revolution* (Savas Beatie, 2007); Williams, John, *The Battle of Hubbardton: The Americans Stem the Tide*. Vermont Division of Historic Preservation, 1988.

Freeman's Farm, Battle of (Saratoga Campaign)

Date: September 19, 1777
Region: Northern Colonies, New York
Commanders: British: Major General John Burgoyne, Major General Friedrich von Riedesel, Brigadier General Simon Fraser; American: Major

General Horatio Gates, Brigadier General Benedict Arnold, and Colonel Daniel Morgan

Time of Day / Length of Action: 12:45 p.m. to nightfall

Weather Conditions: Cold and foggy in the morning; clear and warm by midday

Opposing Forces: British: 6,000; American: 7,000

British Perspective: By September of 1777, Maj. Gen. John Burgoyne's offensive, known today as the Saratoga Campaign, was not going well. His expedition had lost valuable material resources and more than 1,000 casualties. Although he had regained Fort Ticonderoga and Crown Point, and had secured the terrain surrounding Lake Champlain and the outposts of the northern Hudson River Valley, the British were too thinly stretched to be effective while the strength of their opponents was growing in terms of war materiel, unit strength, and morale. Moreover, Burgoyne's subordinates had suffered a humiliating defeat at the Battle of Bennington (August 16, 1777) and forces led by Col. Barry St. Leger in the Mohawk River Valley had returned to Canada. To make matters worse, Burgoyne's problems with logistics and communications worsened with each passing day.

Burgoyne, however, decided to press his operations southward toward Albany, New York, where he hoped to link up with Maj. Gen. William Howe's main British army, which Burgoyne believed was moving northward up the Hudson River from New York City to meet him. Burgoyne's army was moving toward Albany when he received word that General Howe had decided not to move there as planned, but instead had deployed his army to attack Washington and capture Philadelphia. Howe's decision bewildered the rather inflexible Burgoyne, who decided to continue moving south in New York.

On September 13, Burgoyne and 6,000 British troops crossed the Hudson River and halted at Saratoga, New York. By this time most of Burgoyne's Indian scouts had deserted him and British intelligence concerning the location and intentions of enemy forces was woefully inadequate. His supply line, too, was long and inadequate. Burgoyne continued moving southward and from September 16-18, his forces moved within a short distance of the Americans, who had occupied fortifications on Bemis Heights overlooking the Hudson River. Poor communications and inadequate intelligence continued to hamper the British. Burgoyne had no idea he was outnumbered and did not fully understand how the rebels were deployed.

The aggressive-minded Burgoyne decided to move forward from Sword's Farm, four miles north of Bemis Heights, and attack the enemy. He began his advance at 10:00 a.m. on September 19, a three-pronged movement south by southwest. On the right (west) was Brig. Gen. Simon Fraser and 2,000 men. Fraser's orders were to sweep in an arc and clear the fields and byways of Freeman's farm. On the left (east) were Maj. Gens. Friedrich von Riedesel and William Philips with 1,100 men. Their orders were to approach the Americans by marching south along the main road to Bemis Heights, which ran parallel to the Hudson River. Burgoyne rode with the center column, about 1,100 men under Brig. Gen. James Hamilton. The center column moved generally in the same direction as Fraser's wing; Hamilton's movements would be governed by the reactions of the Americans. Although Burgoyne's movement offered tactical flexibility, the massive reconnaissance-in-force would necessarily stumble blindly through the forest in search of the American lines. Burgoyne's center column reached the Freeman cabin about 12:30 p.m., where a halt was called to await word from the remaining columns.

American Perspective: In the summer of 1777, with General Burgoyne cutting a swath southward through western New York, George Washington dispatched key leaders to help Maj. Gen. Philip Schuyler's Northern Department. Forces commanded by Maj. Gen. Benjamin Lincoln and Col. Daniel Morgan joined with Schuyler at Stillwater. In mid-August, within days of the Patriot victories at Bennington and Fort Stanwix, Maj. Gen. Horatio Gates assumed command of the entire Northern Department. The Continental Congress dispatched Gates to replace Schuyler because of political infighting and friction. Gates wisely moved his army to occupy strategic positions on Bemis Heights, adjacent to the Hudson River.

Gates deployed his men within entrenchments along the high ground just west of the Hudson at Bemis Heights, about one mile south of Freeman's Farm. Some 3,000 troops and the majority of his artillery, which overlooked the river, occupied the positions on the east. General Ebenezer Learned and his 2,000 men defended the center of the American positions farther to the northwest at Nielson's Farm. General Benedict Arnold and Col. Daniel Morgan commanded another 2,000 men west and south of Learned. This latter sector was especially vital to the integrity of the American position because the terrain there was higher; if the British captured heights on the western flank, their artillery would be able to force the Americans to flee, just as they had at Fort Ticonderoga.

As Burgoyne's army felt its way toward Freeman's farm and the western approaches to Bemis Heights, Arnold finally convinced Gates to move out and meet him. Morgan's riflemen and Dearing's light infantry, with Arnold in support, advanced and deployed in the forest surrounding the Freeman fields to await the arrival of their foe.

Terrain: Freeman's farm consisted of gently rolling open fields surrounded by forests. Bemis Heights one mile to the south is a natural plateau east of the Hudson River and south of Mill Creek. Militarily this was key terrain that served as a gateway south to Albany, New York. The dense forest surrounding Bemis Heights provided the combatants with stealthy maneuver room as well as cover and concealment. At Bemis Heights, high ground extended north, west, and east, while the south remained flat and open. In the northwestern corner of Bemis Heights was Nielson's farm, a piece of land owned by a Patriot supporter. The fields of fire inherent in the open farmlands were excellent for both small arms and artillery.

The Fighting: At 12:45 p.m., the Americans opened fire from the trees on Burgoyne's advance guard. Morgan's men were expert marksmen. They trained their muskets on the British officers and knocked many out of the fighting early, demoralizing the foot soldiers. Caught in the open, the British were unable to effectively fight back and broke for the rear. Morgan's men gave chase but stopped when they met Hamilton's main force, fell apart, and then regrouped. By 1:00 p.m., Burgoyne had moved his command into the Freeman clearing with the 20th, 62nd, and 21st regiments in line from left to right, and the 9th Regiment behind in reserve.

The battle opened anew with a thunderous exchange that lasted for several hours, with neither side able to gain a decided advantage. More American regiments gave the rebels a decided numerical advantage and forced the British to spread their line thin to avoid being outflanked. Repeated British bayonet charges were thrown back with heavy loss; the 62nd Regiment was especially exposed and suffered terribly. Riedesel, who was leading Burgoyne's left wing near the Hudson River, heard the fighting and learned of the circumstances from a courier. Burgoyne ordered the German to leave men to hold the road and move west to strike the Americans in the flank. Riedesel moved out, reconnoitered the enemy position, and attacked with two companies. Burgoyne renewed his attack as Riedesel struck. Darkness was falling and by this time Arnold was with Gates in the rear. The Americans held for a time before withdrawing to Bemis Heights.

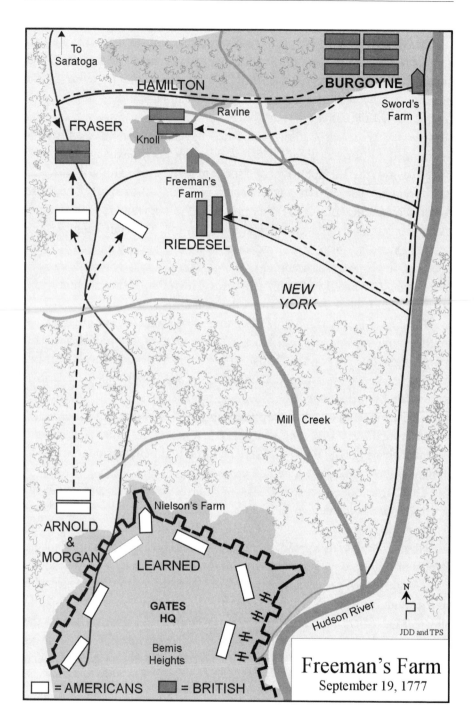

To Saratoga
HAMILTON
BURGOYNE
Sword's Farm
Ravine
FRASER
Knoll
Freeman's Farm
RIEDESEL
NEW YORK
Mill Creek
Nielson's Farm
ARNOLD & MORGAN
LEARNED
GATES HQ
Bemis Heights
Hudson River
N
JDD and TPS

□ = AMERICANS   ■ = BRITISH

Freeman's Farm
September 19, 1777

There are differing accounts of Arnold's role in the fighting. Almost certainly he was present and directing the tactical issues for much of the early action. According to some, he sent a messenger back to Gates requesting reinforcements, but Gates refused and insisted Arnold and Morgan return their men to their assigned defensive positions. Gates's role during the entire affair was defensive-minded. A strong attack from the defenders on the heights in the rear might have caught and easily overwhelmed Burgoyne's dispersed columns. General Learned's brigade had moved out to support the Americans late in the action, but drifted northwest into Fraser's wing, where a brief skirmish erupted that did not contribute to the main combat on the Freeman Farm.

Casualties: British: 600 killed, wounded, and captured; American: 65 killed, 218 wounded, and 36 missing.

Outcome / Impact: Burgoyne occupied the battlefield and could claim a tactical victory. However, the fight eroded British morale and chipped away at his dwindling resources. Because of the wooded terrain and his woeful lack of intelligence, Burgoyne did not yet realize that Gates outnumbered him, and his tactical "victory" that afternoon convinced him to continue moving against his enemy. On the other side of the line, the sharp punch the Americans delivered against Burgoyne's advancing column further emboldened the warrior spirit in the defenders of Bemis Heights. From within their strong positions the rebels awaited the next move of their foe.

Today: Saratoga National Historical Park on the upper Hudson River offers an outstanding visitor center, living history programs, and other cultural and historical activities.

Further Reading: Cook, Fred J., *Dawn Over Saratoga: The Turning Point of the Revolutionary War* (Doubleday, 1973); Ellis, Davis M., *The Saratoga Campaign* (McGraw, 1969); Luzader, John: *Saratoga: A Military History of the Decisive Campaign of the American Revolution* (Savas Beatie, 2007).

British Isles, Battles of the (American Naval Campaign: Europe)

Date: April 1778 – June 1780
Region: Atlantic Ocean (European Theater, naval battles off the coast of the British Isles)
Commanders: British: various; American: Captain John Paul Jones
Time of Day / Length of Action: NA

Weather Conditions: varied

Opposing Forces: British: various; American: various

British Perspective: France's decision to support American independence and its declaration of war against England forced the British to expend considerable resources to defend European waters. Problems between the two nations had been simmering since the end of the Seven Years' War, and in 1778 France believed a new war with England was likely to weaken its longtime enemy and gain the French overseas possessions.

On July 28, 1778, French and British fleets clashed at the First Battle of Ushant, about 100 miles west of a small island of the same name off the northwest corner of France. The British fleet, the vanguard of an amphibious invasion of France, was comprised of 30 warships commanded by Admiral Augustus Keppel. Arrayed against him were 32 French warships under Admiral Louis d'Orvilliers. The battle pitted the finest navies the world's two great sea powers could muster, though the combat was clumsily waged in shifting winds and rain squalls. Both sides lost heavily. French casualties totaled 674, while British losses amounted to 506. The British viewed the battle as a defeat (Keppel was court-martialed, though cleared) because the amphibious assault was turned away.

France's entry made it easier for other nations hungry to nibble at England's empire to follow suit. Spain declared war on England in 1779 and the Dutch followed suit in 1780. The American Revolution, or at least the ripple effects of the war in the colonies, was now a global affair. The French joined with Spain to plan an ambitious offensive against the British home isles, but after careful planning the invasion was never launched. The British were now fighting four countries (Spain, France, Holland, and America), and their military capabilities were stretched thin. Her enemies exploited the Crown's attenuated condition by grabbing territory and resources around the world wherever and whenever they could, which in turn kept the British fleet and military resources busy and away from the American colonies.

American Perspective: By 1777 the nascent Continental fleet was barely worthy of the name. The colonists had few resources with which to construct and maintain a credible fleet and no one harbored illusions that anything the Americans could float would counter the British head-to-head. Aggravating efforts to build a navy were the individual states themselves, which focused maritime resources on maintaining their own respective state navies. These "mosquito fleets," comprised of converted merchant ships and prize vessels, were dedicated to the defense of their respective shores.

Though limited in number, the few ships of the Continental fleet remained engaged throughout the war in varying degrees of service. In June of 1777, Capt. John Paul Jones was given command of *Ranger*, which he sailed to France. Jones's mission was to inform French authorities that General Burgoyne had surrendered his army at Saratoga—a critical victory that helped convince the French to ally with America. Jones took several prize vessels en route to European shores, and while in France devised a plan to raid shipping around the British Isles. Jones set sail on April 11, 1778, and in the Irish Sea off the west coast of England captured several merchant ships. Following successful small raids on English soil, Jones captured the 20-gun HMS *Drake* in America's first conventional naval battle.

While the American naval campaign was nothing more than a hit and run affair through British home waters, the news of Jones's success bolstered morale back home. *Ranger* returned to America under a different captain. Jones remained in France to work with Ambassador Benjamin Franklin and assist French authorities in refitting an old ship into a man-of-war. The converted 40-gun warship was called *Bonhomme Richard* in honor of Benjamin Franklin. With additional assistance from the French government, Jones built a small squadron around *Bonhomme Richard* and put to sea on August 14, 1779. Jones's fleet captured several ships. On September 23 he engaged in what is probably the best-known ship-to-ship battle of the revolution when *Bonhomme Richard* defeated HMS *Serapis* in the North Sea. In June of 1780, Louis XVI presented Jones with a sword engraved with the phrase "To the valiant avenger of the rights of the sea."

Terrain: The British Isles and the waters in which John Paul Jones conducted his campaign lie in the North Atlantic surrounding Ireland in the west, Scotland in the north, and England in the east. Jones sailed about 1,700 miles on his first cruise into the Irish Sea. He left Brest, France, in the Bay of Biscay and sailed up Ireland's east coast, eventually stopping on the west coast of England (Battle of Whitehaven) before continuing northward around Ireland (Battle with *Drake*). He sailed along the west coast of that country before returning to port at Brest. Jones's second voyage began at Lorient, France, another Biscay port. This time he made a broad arc around the west coast of Ireland, moving north by northeast to the coast of Scotland, and south along the east coast of that country. He continued sailing in a southerly direction to the east coast of England (battle with *Serapis*) before seeking a safe port in Holland.

The Fighting: (Raids on Whitehaven, England, and St. Mary's Island, Scotland) During his cruise around the eastern shores of England, Captain

Jones personally led a little-known raid on a British fort at Whitehaven on April 22, 1778. The daring amphibious assault conducted at dawn succeeded in surprising the small garrison and taking the stronghold without firing a shot. Jones knew he would not be able to hold the fort, but that was never his intent. Instead, he spiked 36 heavy cannons and destroyed several British ships in the nearby harbor before sailing away. The next day Jones and his men raided Scotland's St. Mary's Island, where they unsuccessfully attempted to kidnap the Earl of Selkirk. Jones had hoped to use the valuable hostage to negotiate the exchange of American sailors held by the British in England. When the plan failed he continued his cruise around the eastern coast of England.

(*Ranger* vs. *Drake*) The British dispatched several warships to capture the irksome rebel raiders terrorizing the British home islands. On April 24, 1778, British man-of-war *Drake* approached the *Ranger* off Carrickfergus, Ireland. Rather foolishly, the British captain sent a boat out to inquire the nationality of *Ranger*; Jones promptly captured it. Cleared for action, *Drake* eased closer to *Ranger* and hailed the ship. Jones (or his first officer, depending upon the source) responded, "This is the American Continental ship *Ranger*, we wait for you, and beg you will come on. The sun is little more than an hour high, and it is time to begin!" After taunting the enemy Jones initiated the battle by sending a broadside into the British ship. About one hour later *Drake* struck her colors and surrendered. Jones lost only two killed and six wounded, while the British suffered 45 killed and wounded. Jones was hailed a hero when he returned to France with his prizes, which he had to sell to feed and pay his near-mutinous crew.

(*Bonhomme Richard* vs. *Serapis*) Jones's small fleet captured more than a dozen prize ships en route to a designated rendezvous site off the coasts of England and Scotland. Several of his ships failed to arrive. While waiting for them at Flamborough Head on September 23, 1779, the 44-gun British frigate *Serapis* and 22-gun *Countess of Scarborough* cruised into range escorting a fleet of 40 merchant ships. Jones attacked the British at sunset under a rising full moon. The dramatic and bitterly contested duel consumed four hours. The struggle between *Bonhomme Richard* and *Serapis* (and to a lesser degree, *Countess of Scarborough*) was as much brawl as masterful seamanship. The two ships repeatedly unloaded broadsides into each other's hulls, cutting rigging, puncturing sails, and killing and maiming sailors. When one of the shots dropped the American flag, British commander Capt. Richard Pearson asked Jones if he intended to surrender. Jones, in one of the

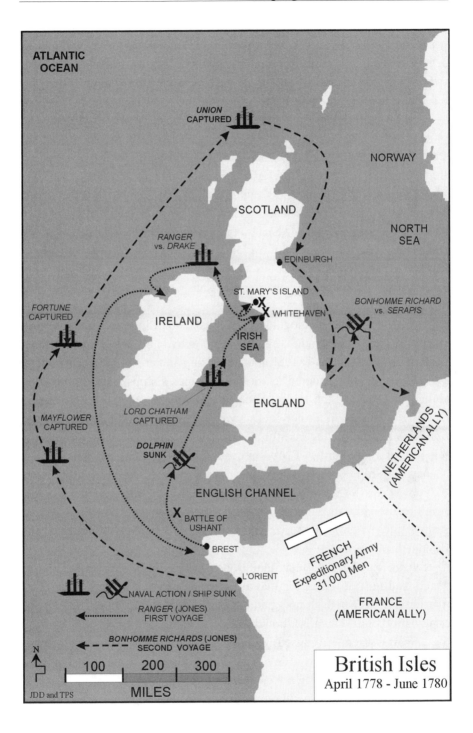

ATLANTIC
OCEAN

UNION
CAPTURED

NORWAY

SCOTLAND

NORTH
SEA

RANGER
vs. DRAKE

EDINBURGH

ST. MARY'S ISLAND

FORTUNE
CAPTURED

BONHOMME RICHARD
vs. SERAPIS

WHITEHAVEN

IRELAND

IRISH
SEA

ENGLAND

NETHERLANDS
(AMERICAN ALLY)

LORD CHATHAM
CAPTURED

MAYFLOWER
CAPTURED

DOLPHIN
SUNK

ENGLISH CHANNEL

BATTLE OF
USHANT

BREST

FRENCH
Expeditionary Army
31,000 Men

L'ORIENT

NAVAL ACTION / SHIP SUNK

FRANCE
(AMERICAN ALLY)

RANGER (JONES)
FIRST VOYAGE

BONHOMME RICHARDS (JONES)
SECOND VOYAGE

N

100   200   300

MILES

JDD and TPS

British Isles
April 1778 - June 1780

war's most famous phrases, supposedly replied, "Surrender? I have not yet begun to fight!" According to Jones, however, his answer was a bit less artful: "That point didn't occur to me, but I am determined to make you ask for quarter!"

As the battle dragged on *Bonhomme Richard* lost both rigging and rudder, but when *Serapis* moved alongside to deliver a final blow, she strayed too close and her jib boom became entangled with the American ship. Jones's men threw grappling hooks onto *Serapis* and lashed her fast. This act effectively removed *Countess of Scarborough* from the action because her captain did not want to risk hitting *Serapis*. Hand grenades were tossed into the *Serapis's* hold, slaughtering dozens of British sailors. Hundreds of captured British sailors held prisoner aboard *Bonhomme Richard* were released with Jones's permission, but most were set to work manning pumps to keep the badly hulled ship from sinking. The battle was but half finished.

With the ships lashed together, Jones led a boarding party onto *Serapis*, where the combatants fought hand-to-hand above and below decks. About 10:30 p.m. Pearson finally surrendered his ship and crew to Jones. *Countess of Scarborough* surrendered to another of Jones's ships a short time later. Hulled and listing, the badly damaged *Bonhomme Richard* was clearly mortally wounded. With her decks awash with blood and mangled bodies, *Bonhomme Richard* lingered for two days before losing her battle with the sea. Half of Jones's crew of 240 was dead or wounded. Jones took *Serapis* as his new flagship.

Casualties: (*Ranger* vs. *Drake*): British: 42 killed and wounded; American: eight killed and wounded; (*Bonhomme Richard* vs. *Serapis*): British: 600 killed, wounded, and captured; American: 120 killed and wounded.

Outcome / Impact: John Paul Jones's expedition into British home waters had no impact on the overall outcome of the war, though his raid interfered with British shipping and caused considerable consternation. His exploits inflicted several million dollars of damage to British shipping, and the embarrassment he caused his enemy helped boost American morale. Jones's attack on the fort at Whitehaven was the only time Americans set foot on English soil during the Revolutionary War.

In addition to the expeditions of John Paul Jones and the French naval battles fought around the British Isles, other European sea battles played a role in tying up British military resources in waters far from American shores. Because the colonial war was now a global conflict, one of the possessions England was forced to heavily guard was Gibraltar, the strategic guardian of the entrance of the Mediterranean Sea. On October 20, 1782, an allied Franco-Spanish fleet made up of 46 ships of the line fought for control of Gibraltar against 35 British warships under Admiral Sir Richard Howe. The four-hour Battle of Cape Spartel off the coast of Morocco ended in British success, with each side suffering about 600 casualties.

Further Reading: Dupuy, Trevor Nevitt, *The Military History of Revolutionary War Naval Battles* (Franklin Watts, Inc., 1970); Allen, Gardner, *A Naval History of the American Revolution* (Houghton, 1913).

Caribbean, Battles of the (Naval Campaign: Caribbean)

Date: February 1778–April 1782
Region: Atlantic Ocean (Naval and land battles fought in the Caribbean Sea)
Commanders: British: Various; American and French: Various
Time of Day / Length of Action: NA
Weather Conditions: NA
Opposing Forces: Various
British Perspective: Throughout the American Revolution, England faced serious challenges to its substantial interests in the Caribbean. Beginning on March 3, 1776, when Americans seized British forts at Nassau in the Bahamas, the Crown was forced to commit men and resources to the defense of its West Indies colonies. The nascent American navy was too small to maintain control of territory beyond its borders or directly threaten England at sea, so colonial naval threats did not overly preoccupy England's military commanders. All of this changed in 1778 when the French recognized America and joined the war. The move forced the British to commit fleets and permanent garrisons to the West Indies lest they lose their island colonies to the French. In 1779 and 1780, Spain and Holland, respectively, joined the war as American allies. Both were naval powers. The threat to British sovereignty in the West Indies was at a crisis point.

From 1778 to 1782 the British continuously reinforced their Caribbean forts, committed a permanent military presence in the islands, and posted large numbers of warships there to guard island territories. Occasional enemy raids into the region from 1778 through 1780 were successfully defended. However, in 1781 and 1782, as the war in America drew to a close, France and Spain attacked the weakened but still powerful British with their full strength. As the French and Spanish discovered, the British navy still ruled the seas. When the fighting was over England's possessions were still under the Union Jack.

American Perspective: The small Continental Navy launched successful small-scale raids of British possessions in the Caribbean, but the risk to the enemy was irksome at best. The tiny American squadrons faced great peril as the British steadily increased the military strength of her island colonies. By 1780 the shattered American fleet consisted primarily of borrowed vessels and tiny state-run squadrons that could do little more than capture foreign merchant vessels as prizes. However, American allies actively engaged British interests with increasing frequency and strength, and from an American perspective, every action that forced the British to employ resources away from the colonies was a success. After the surrender of Cornwallis at Yorktown in October 1781, America's allies moved the thrust of their war with Great Britain to distant shores. In the Caribbean, French and Spanish fleets attacked the British, though without lasting success.

Terrain: The Caribbean consists of the Caribbean Sea, which is a part of the North Atlantic Ocean and the islands located therein, including Antigua, Barbuda, Bahamas, Cuba, Dominica, Dominican Republic, Grenada, Haiti, Trinidad, Tobago, Jamaica, St. Lucia, St. Kitts, Nevis, and St. Vincent. These primary islands are commonly known as the West Indies. In the 18th century, several empires wrestled for control of these islands, including France, Great Britain, Spain, and Holland. The islands were prized for their resources and for their strategic location as ports and colonies. The name Caribbean is derived from the Carib people who originally inhabited the area at the time of its discovery by Spanish explorers in the 15th Century.

The sea is roughly 1,500 miles (east to west) by 1,400 miles (north to south), or roughly 1,050,000 square miles. Its major shipping lane was the Windward Passage between Haiti and Cuba. Its boundary to the north and east is the West Indies, South America to the south, and Central America to the west. The Gulf of Mexico lies to the northwest, connecting with the Caribbean Sea via a 120-mile wide corridor between Cuba and the Yucatan Peninsula of Mexico. The sea was generally easy to navigate, offered mild tides, and tropical weather. The equatorial currents provided excellent sailing via a predominantly northwestern flow. However, hurricanes also followed this track from June to November.

The Fighting: *2nd Raid on Nassau*: In January 1778, the Americans conducted several operations in Caribbean waters. The frigate *Providence* returned to the Bahamas and helped capture British forts in Nassau on January 27, seize 1,600 pounds of gunpowder, and free 30 American prisoners of war being held on the island. The effort also recaptured five American ships and captured a 16-gun British sloop. This raid was nearly a replay of a previous assault in 1776, only much more successful. After returning to America, *Providence* captured prize ships along the coast of New England until she was destroyed at the Battle of Penobscot Bay (August 14, 1779).

Randolph vs. *Yarmouth*: On February 12, 1778, the American frigate *Randolph* and four South Carolina ships commanded by Capt. Nicholas Biddle cruised into the Caribbean Sea in search of prize vessels. Instead of easy prizes, however, on March 7, 1778, the little American squadron ran squarely into *Yarmouth*, a 64-gun British ship-of-the-line. *Yarmouth* was twice its size and boasted twice as many guns, but the faster *Randolph* heroically (some might say foolishly) closed for battle. Captain Biddle fired first and the British quickly returned fire. Although Biddle's shots ripped apart *Yarmouth's* rigging and sails, *Randolph* exploded and sank with 311 men, including the promising young Captain Biddle. In all likelihood a lucky shot had penetrated *Randolph's* magazine. Biddle's well-handled guns, however, heavily damaged *Yarmouth*, which had to put in for repairs in Jamaica before sailing for Portsmouth. She never saw combat service again.

Battles of Martinique, St. Lucia, and Tobago: In 1781, a French fleet led by Admiral François Joseph Paul Comte de Grasse sailed for the island of Martinique, where it clashed with a British fleet commanded by Rear Admiral Samuel Hood. The British valiantly attempted to keep the French from reaching their port at Fort de France, but were unsuccessful. De Grasse tried to land 1,200 marines to take the island of St. Lucia, but the British succeeded in knocking back the effort. Stymied, the French fleet moved on to Tobago, which was seized on July 26, 1781. De Grasse next sailed his French warships to Haiti, where they joined forces with another squadron commanded by Rear Admiral Comte de Guichen. Together they sailed for the coast of Virginia to assist Washington's Franco-American army against Cornwallis. On September 5, the French fleet engaged a British fleet

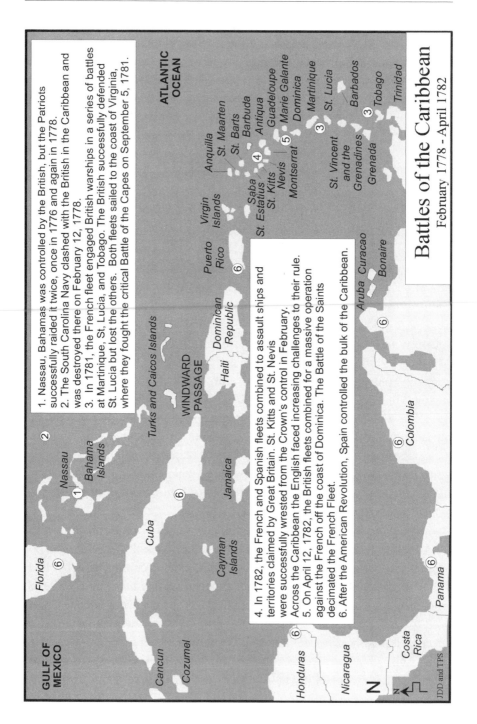

Battles of the Caribbean
February 1778 - April 1782

1. Nassau, Bahamas was controlled by the British, but the Patriots successfully raided it twice, once in 1776 and again in 1778.

2. The South Carolina Navy clashed with the British in the Caribbean and was destroyed there on February 12, 1778.

3. In 1781, the French fleet engaged British warships in a series of battles at Martinique, St, Lucia, and Tobago. The British successfully defended St. Lucia but lost the others. Both fleets sailed to the coast of Virginia, where they fought the critical Battle of the Capes on September 5, 1781.

4. In 1782, the French and Spanish fleets combined to assault ships and territories claimed by Great Britain. St. Kitts and St. Nevis were successfully wrested from the Crown's control in February. Across the Caribbean the English faced increasing challenges to their rule.

5. On April 12, 1782, the British fleets combined for a massive operation against the French off the coast of Dominica. The Battle of the Saints decimated the French Fleet.

6. After the American Revolution, Spain controlled the bulk of the Caribbean.

ATLANTIC OCEAN

GULF OF MEXICO

Florida ⑥

Cancun

Cozumel

Cuba

Bahama Islands

Nassau ①

②

Turks and Caicos Islands

WINDWARD PASSAGE

Haiti

Dominican Republic

Jamaica ⑥

Cayman Islands

Honduras ⑥

Nicaragua

Costa Rica ⑥

Panama

Colombia ⑥

Aruba Curacao Bonaire ⑥

Puerto Rico ⑥

Virgin Islands

Saba St. Estatius

St. Kitts Nevis Montserrat

Anguilla St. Maarten St. Barts Barbuda Antigua Guadeloupe Marie Galante Dominica Martinique St. Lucia Barbados Tobago ③ Trinidad

④

⑤

③

St. Vincent and the Grenadines Grenada ③

N

JDD and TPS

commanded by Rear Admiral Thomas Graves at the Battle of the Capes. The combat was the decisive naval battle of the American Revolution. The French victory drove away Graves's fleet and secured the Chesapeake Bay for the Allied siege of Yorktown, Virginia, which ultimately forced the surrender of Cornwallis's army and the end of the war.

Battles of St. Kitts and Nevis: In late 1781 and 1782, with the war virtually over in America and treaty negotiations underway, the French and Spanish continued fighting the British. On November 5, 1781, a strong French fleet of 29 ships under de Grasse returned to the Caribbean and successfully captured the islands of St. Kitts and Nevis. On January 25, 1782, Admiral Samuel Hood's inferior force recaptured the harbor and waged what is largely recognized as the finest example of British military seamanship of the war, but the British post on St. Kitts surrendered to the French on February 12. The French rolled up the islands and after two months of campaigning the British had nearly lost control of the Caribbean.

Battle of the Saints / Iles de Saintes: After de Grasse's victory at St. Kitts and Nevis, he planned to join his warships with the Spanish fleet and, in a massive joint operation, attack British-held Jamaica. The British were equally determined to prevent a link up of their two main enemies and attacked the French before they could get into position to strike. Admirals George Rodney and Samuel Hood combined their fleets and the large British armada struck the French on April 12, 1782, near the Dominican coast at Iles de Saintes. Known as the Battle of the Saints, 36 British ships of the line squared off against a French fleet of 33 warships. The French were out maneuvered and outfought and many of de Grasse's ships ran out of ammunition. Badly beaten, the French fleet was captured or destroyed and 6,000 men lost their lives. Admiral de Grasse surrendered *Le Ville de Paris*, his 130-gun flagship and the pride of his fleet. The surviving French warships sought shelter at their port in Haiti. The bloody battle ended French efforts against the British in the Caribbean. It also marked the end of major naval combat during the American Revolution.

Casualties: Known casualty data has been included in the narrative above.

Outcome / Impact: The impact of these battles was primarily realized in their collateral assistance rendered to the American cause by forcing the British to focus on areas beyond the colonies. The battles also provided for a division of the island colonies in the Caribbean.

Further Reading: Dupuy, Trevor Nevitt, *The Military History of Revolutionary War Naval Battles* (Franklin Watts, Inc., 1970); Allen, Gardner, *A Naval History of the American Revolution* (Houghton, 1913).

Charleston, Siege of (Southern Campaign)

Date: April 18, 1780 – May 12, 1780

Region: Southern Colonies, South Carolina

Commanders: British: Lieutenant General Sir Henry Clinton, Lieutenant General Charles Cornwallis, Admiral Mariot Arbuthnot, Major General Augustine Prevost; American: Major General Benjamin Lincoln, Brigadier General Isaac Huger, and Brigadier General William Moultrie

Time of Day / Length of Action: Siege: Three weeks; Battle of Monck's Corner: 3:00 p.m. to 4:00 p.m.

Weather Conditions: Typical mild, Spring weather

Opposing Forces: British: 13,500; American: 7,000

British Perspective: Following Maj. Gen. Augustine Prevost's victory at Savannah (September-October 1779), Lt. Gen. Henry Clinton decided to attack Charleston a second time and invest more resources in the Southern Theater of operations. Clinton was keenly aware of the failed previous attempt to take Charleston on June 28, 1776, and that the earlier operation had consisted of a maritime assault against strong Patriot fortifications erected on Sullivan's Island. With a stalemate in the Northern Theater, Crown authorities decreed the major effort to win the war would be undertaken in the South, where it was believed better opportunities for long-term strategic success could be found. Many believed Loyalist support there would turn decisively in England's favor with a significant victory similar to Prevost's Savannah operations. Charleston was believed to be the key to obtaining that high-profile success.

British naval elements spent the months of December 1779 and January 1780 battling storms and moving through frigid winds to reach Savannah. The fleet was comprised of 90 troop carriers and 14 warships. The stormy seas delayed the effort and at one point dispersed the fleet. The British assault troops did not set foot in Georgia until February 4, 1780. The first units ashore included Lt. Col. Banastre Tarleton's infamous cavalry and the Loyalist Provincials led by Maj. Patrick Ferguson. These men would later play key roles in several battles. They moved their horsemen north to attack and harass Charleston by land. The British Fleet, meanwhile, sailed northward for Charleston. The main army disembarked at Seabrook Island, well south of the city, while the fleet sailed on to Johns Island, just a few miles below Charleston, on February 11, 1780. During the course of the next few weeks the army moved on to James Island and Wappoo Cut, inching closer to Charleston. The fleet followed the troops northward along the inter-coastal waterways, providing supplies to keep the large army fed and equipped. Americans harassed the British during the approach to the outskirts of Charleston, but the large British force simply pushed them aside and continued its offensive.

Moving steadily northward, the British crossed the Ashley River and marched east toward Charleston Neck from the mainland of South Carolina. Clinton's line stretched for about one and one-half miles across the peninsula, its flanks anchored on the Ashley and Charles rivers. On April 2 the British began building formal siege lines in the time-honored European fashion. The British fleet also made its presence off the Charleston bar.

American Perspective: The move against Charleston posed significant and largely insurmountable problems for Maj. Gen. Benjamin Lincoln, the commander of the American Southern Department. He had only 3,600 men available when operations commenced, his few forts were not prepared for action, and his navy was hardly worthy of the name. When the British landed troops at Johns Island on February 11, Lt. Col. Francis Marion, commander of the city's southern defenses, warned his leaders in Charleston of the impending danger and used his small force of mounted "swamp fighters" to harass the British. Nothing Marion could do would stop the scarlet juggernaut. Panic gripped the city when the British army marched inland and threatened it with capture from west of Charleston Neck. Offshore, the huge British fleet threatened the small American navy. Its commander, Commodore Abraham Whipple, scuttled most of his vessels along with a few merchant ships at the mouth of the harbor in the Cooper River to obstruct that waterway. In an effort to mount a credible defense of the city, Lincoln lashed out at the British siege lines on Charleston Neck and opened fire with a long and occasionally effective cannonade.

Lincoln's problems were multiplied when smallpox broke out in Charleston, local militia organizations provided faulty intelligence, and Spain refused to send assistance. Worse still, the French had virtually abandoned the Americans after the fiasco at Savannah. South Carolina's first Patriot Governor, John Rutledge, assumed dictatorial powers to control the growing chaos in Charleston.

On April 6, Brig. Gen. William Woodford arrived in Charleston with 750 reinforcements from Virginia and North Carolina after a 28-day forced march. Unfortunately, there was little additional troops could do to save the city. The British war machine was steadily tightening its vice-like grip on the citadel of the south, and there were not nearly enough Patriot troops in position to stop it. On April 9, fourteen British warships crossed the sandbar, exchanged fire with the artillery from Fort Moultrie, and successfully entered Charleston harbor. The next day Clinton asked Lincoln to surrender the city, an offer Lincoln flatly refused. It was obvious, however, that unless something completely unexpected occurred, capitulation was only a matter of time. In an effort to save the state's political apparatus, Governor Rutledge and other public officials were secreted outside Charleston on April 13 to reestablish the government elsewhere.

Terrain: The port city of Charleston sits on a peninsula at the conflux of the Cooper, Wando, and Ashley rivers, all of which empty into Charleston harbor and the Atlantic Ocean. This terrain forms a natural harbor surrounded by marshy lowlands and shifting sand bars. The harbor entrance is narrow and shallow, and at its entrance is a large sand bar that in the 18th century was not passable during low tide; at high tide there were only five channels through which ships could pass safely into and out of the harbor. The peninsula on the land side was flat, sandy, and marshy.

The Fighting: On April 12, Clinton ordered Colonel Tarleton to ride behind and north of Charleston and sever its communications with the rest of South Carolina by land. With Maj. Patrick Ferguson and his men, Tarleton rode out on the night of April 13 toward the important logistical and communications strong point at Monck's Corner, about 30 miles distant. Defending Monck's Corner was Brig. Gen. Isaac Huger and 500 mounted militia. Lincoln had ordered Huger to hold the critical crossroads and supply depot at all costs. On the way to their objective the British cavalry intercepted an American courier with a message detailing the strength and disposition of Huger's troops.

At 3:00 a.m. on April 14, Tarleton launched his troops in a rapid assault that utterly defeated the unsuspecting Americans. Tarleton's Monck's Corner victory cut off Charleston's communications, captured scores of wagons and horses, and burnished his image as an outstanding raider-tactician. Huger and most of his men managed to escape, but more than two dozen were killed and wounded. According to Tarleton, who lost

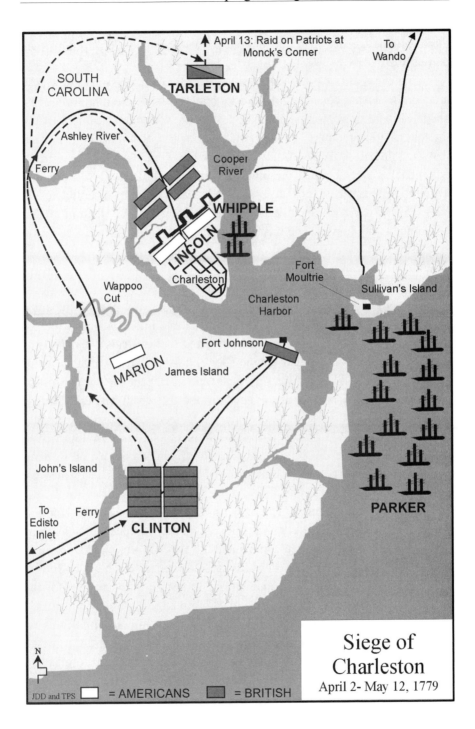

April 13: Raid on Patriots at Monck's Corner

To Wando

SOUTH CAROLINA

TARLETON

Ashley River

Ferry

Cooper River

WHIPPLE

LINCOLN

Charleston

Fort Moultrie

Sullivan's Island

Wappoo Cut

Charleston Harbor

Fort Johnson

MARION

James Island

John's Island

To Edisto Inlet   Ferry

CLINTON

PARKER

N

JDD and TPS   ☐ = AMERICANS   ☐ = BRITISH

Siege of Charleston
April 2- May 12, 1779

three wounded, Huger had not sent out proper patrols or deployed his men correctly.

After the April 14 fight at the strategic crossroads, the next few weeks around Charleston consisted of artillery duels, small-scale infantry sorties, and traditional siege methodology. Fort Moultrie surrendered on May 6 with the loss of 200 prisoners. Two days later General Clinton again demanded that Lincoln surrender. Negotiations began, but were eventually broken off when each officer blamed the other of violating the agreed-to cease fire. Throughout this period local citizens pleaded with Lincoln to capitulate. On May 11 British "hot shot" artillery fire triggered a conflagration that consumed many homes. The following day Lincoln surrendered Charleston and his army.

Casualties: British: 78 killed and 189 wounded; American: 89 killed, 138 wounded, and 6,684 soldiers and sailors captured.

Outcome / Impact: The siege of Charleston was one of the most disastrous American defeats of the entire Revolution. Along with the thousands of men who laid down their arms to the British, the Patriots forfeited 154 cannons, tons of gunpowder and food, and yet another major southern port city. The loss was significant and its impact, including a loss of confidence in the Patriot cause, echoed around the world. General Lincoln and most of his senior officers were later exchanged for British officers, but many of the Regular Continental line soldiers and sailors were imprisoned and died miserable deaths aboard British prison ships. Major General Horatio Gates was placed in command of the remnants of the American Southern Department.

The victory convinced General Clinton that his theory the colonies could be rolled up from south to north was viable. In order to conduct this operation, Clinton transferred command of all British forces in the Southern colonies to Lt. Gen. Charles Cornwallis and returned to New York on June 5, 1780. Cornwallis had explicit instructions to secure the Carolinas for the Crown and march north toward Virginia. Clinton, meanwhile, would return to New York and sweep southward from that point, the generals crushing what was left of the rebellion between them.

By June of 1780, the British controlled Georgia from Augusta to Savannah. In South Carolina they established outposts, offered paroles to rebels, and lucrative enlistments to the local Tories. One of Clinton's biggest mistakes was his decision to free those American militiamen who had sworn allegiance to the King. This distasteful demand was intolerable to the Patriot warriors, who returned to the field after their release and continued fighting.

Today: The Monck's Corner field remains in private hands. Little in the way of the siege of Charleston discussed in this entry remains, although historical plaques and markers can be found throughout the city and its surrounding countryside.

Further Reading: Borick, Carl P., *A Gallant Defense: The Siege of Charleston, 1780* (University of South Carolina Press, 2003); Gordon, John W., *South Carolina and the American Revolution: A Battlefield History* (University of South Carolina Press, 2003); Lumpkin, Henry, *From Savannah to Yorktown: The American Revolution in the South* (Paragon House, 1981).

Cowpens, Battle of (Southern Campaign)

Date: January 17, 1781

Region: Southern Colonies, South Carolina

Commanders: British: Lieutenant General Charles Cornwallis and Colonel Banastre Tarleton; American: Major General Nathanael Greene, Brigadier General Daniel Morgan, Colonel Andrew Pickens, Lieutenant Colonels John Howard and William Washington, Majors John McDowell and John Cunningham

Time of Day / Length of Action: 7:00 a.m. to 8:00 a.m.

Weather Conditions: Cold, clear, and sunny

Opposing Forces: British: 1,100; American: 1,065

British Perspective: During the winter of 1780-1781, General Charles Cornwallis's army remained in cold weather quarters at Winnsboro, South Carolina. His ranks were swelled by an additional 2,000 troops from the Northern colonies. His soldiers actively patrolled the countryside around Winnsboro in order to keep rebel raiding parties led by Thomas Sumter and Francis Marion away from slow moving British supply trains. Lieutenant Colonel Banastre Tarleton's cavalry patrolled the western upcountry region of the state. On November 20, 1780, Tarleton encountered and narrowly defeated Sumter's rebel army at Blackstock's Plantation. The cavalry leader fought his command piecemeal against a rebel army that outnumbered his own by nearly four-to-one. The result was nearly disastrous for the British, who suffered heavy casualties in the expensive tactical victory.

When Cornwallis learned in early January 1781 that Gen. Daniel Morgan was operating in the western part of the state, he dispatched Tarleton to find and defeat them. Gathering intelligence along the way, Tarleton pursued the rebels northward toward Cowpens, South Carolina, a few miles below the North Carolina border. Tarleton reported the rebel position and Cornwallis maneuvered part of his main army northwest to help Tarleton trap Morgan's Americans.

After the bloody lesson Sumter taught him at Blackstock's Plantation, Tarleton maintained a tighter rein on his troops. With his 1,100-man army and two small-bore artillery pieces, the British cavalry leader approached Morgan's rebels from the southeast along Mill Gap (now Green River) Road. Tarleton had pushed his army through most of a long cold night's journey of 12 miles before catching up with Morgan at Cowpens about 6:30 a.m. on January 17.

American Perspective: In 1780, two battles played a major role in changing America's Southern war strategy. The first was Camden (August 16), where tremendous losses embarrassed the Patriot cause and shattered the Continental Army's Southern Department. The second was at Kings Mountain (October 7), where a determined attack by a group of frontiersmen wiped out a 1,000-man Loyalist command and collapsed Cornwallis's bid to invade North Carolina. The victory revealed for the world that the British were indeed vulnerable, and offered a sliver of hope to the beleaguered rebel cause.

That setback notwithstanding, Gen. George Washington knew if Cornwallis continued moving north unchecked the Americans would be crushed between two giant British pincer arms (Cornwallis from the south and Gen. Henry Clinton from the north). Appreciating that the Southern Department was vital to the Patriot cause, and cognizant that good leadership could bring about more victories like Kings Mountain, Washington transferred key commanders and units to the Carolinas to rescue a war effort that was in real danger of foundering.

On October 30, Gen. Nathanael Greene replaced Camden's disgraced Horatio Gates as the commander of the Southern Department. One of Washington's most trusted veteran leaders, Greene quickly reorganized and revitalized the shattered command. Washington also promoted Virginian Daniel Morgan, one of his most dependable fighters and experienced backwoodsmen. Morgan and his rangers had successfully conducted Indian-style raids and stood the trials of traditional combat for years against

Britain's finest soldiers. By making Morgan a brigadier general, Washington offered the Patriot cause a fighting leader the rank and file would willingly fight hard and die for. Morgan was aggressive, experienced, wise, and a natural combat officer—exactly what the Southern Department needed. Washington also transferred Lt. Col. Henry Lee and his cavalry corps of 350 men to the Carolinas.

Greene boldly divided his small army to better harass the British over a wider region. The general remained with the wing operating around an enemy outpost at Camden. With Greene's second wing, Morgan was ordered to operate against Ninety Six. Between these two positions were Cornwallis and 4,000 men at Winnsboro. Greene's bold plan risked a decisive move by Cornwallis against either Greene or Morgan, and thus a defeat in detail.

Morgan made camp on the Pacolet River along the border of North Carolina and South Carolina. When Cornwallis learned about Morgan's potentially exposed position, he ordered Tarleton and his light troops and dragoons to destroy him. On January 13, 1781, Lt. Col. William Washington's cavalry was patrolling the vicinity of Fair Forest when they came upon a large band of Tories. The cavalry captured 40 prisoners and derived intelligence from them (and local inhabitants) that British troops were operating nearby at Musgrove's Mill. Morgan wisely maneuvered his forces away from his enemy until he reached the Broad River just below the North Carolina border at a local gathering place known as "Hannah's Cowpens."

Morgan decided to give battle at Cowpens because the position offered advantageous terrain for the type of combat he intended to wage against Tarleton. It was also a well known and easy gathering place, though an impassable river meandered five miles behind his rear. With him were about 1,000 soldiers (533 militiamen from Virginia, Georgia, and both Carolinas, 237 Continentals, 80 cavalrymen, and about 200 independent riflemen; estimates vary from 800 to 1,065). Morgan set about arranging his command into a clever deployment.

Some 150 militia riflemen were placed in front as a skirmish line under Maj. John McDowell and Maj. John Cunningham, the Green River (Mill Gap) Road dividing the line. The militiamen were outstanding marksmen but were not known as dependable front line soldiers. Knowing this, Morgan asked that they fire twice and retire firing back to the second line 150 yards to their rear. He knew he could not get much else out of his militia, and this arrangement would maximize their firepower and keep them in place if they knew they could retire quickly instead of having to stand and face British steel. The battle line the militiamen would fall back to reinforce 150 yards to the northwest was under the command of Col. Andrew Pickens. This second line, resting on the field's military crest, was comprised of 300 militia. Morgan had cautioned these men the night before to wait until the British were within easy range, aim at the officers, and then after two shots or "hits" retire around the left flank of the third or final line, where they could reform.

Lieutenant Colonel John Howard and his 450 riflemen (mostly Continentals) held the last line, a slightly higher position 150 yards behind Pickens. This base formation was flanked on both sides by 200 independent Virginia riflemen whose shooting skills were unsurpassed. William Washington (the general's cousin) and his cavalry were placed in the rear as a reserve beyond the range of both enemy fire and easy observation.

Terrain: The rolling Cowpens battlefield is four miles east of Chesnee, South Carolina, and 28 miles due west of Kings Mountain. The elevation at the highest point on the battlefield is 296 feet, and the region is drained by the Broad River, which flows from northwest to southeast five miles behind where Morgan took up his position. Divided by the Mill Gap Road, the battlefield was essentially a broad pasture one-half mile wide (southwest to northeast) and one mile long (southeast to northwest). Light timber dotted the landscape, which was used to graze cattle (hence the name Cowpens). The terrain rises gently from southeast (British approach) to northwest (American defensive positions). Thickety Mountain is visible to the southeast, and the Blue Ridge Mountains rise in the north and dominate the horizon.

The Fighting: Pleased the Americans had decided to stand and fight, Tarleton arranged for immediate battle. He did not believe the terrain offered any special advantage to his opponent, and Morgan's flanks were not properly anchored. With an air of impatience Tarleton formed his tired command for battle with the 7th Regiment of Foot on the left and three light infantry companies extending the line to the right across the road. Two detachments of dragoons, about 50 in each, were posted to the flanks, one on each side. Tarleton formed his 280 light cavalry behind the main line, and on the left center unlimbered his pair of guns, one on either side of the Legion infantry. In his left rear was the 71st Highlander Regiment. So formed, the impetuous British commander ordered his men to charge the American lines. It was about 7:00 a.m.

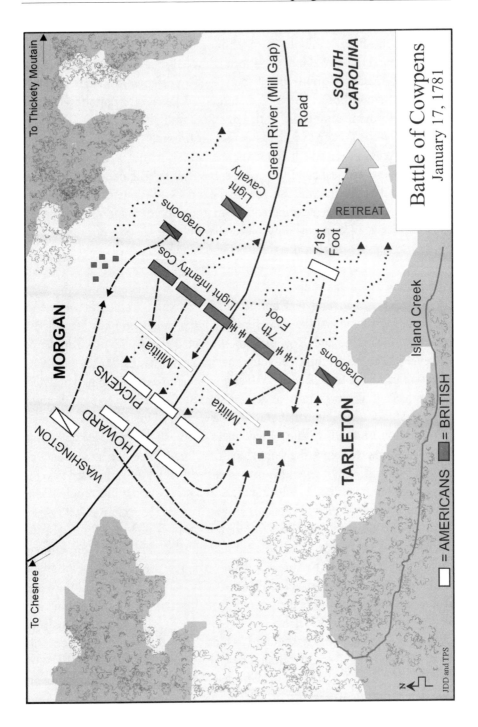

Battle of Cowpens
January 17, 1781

To Thickety Moutain

Green River (Mill Gap)

Road

SOUTH CAROLINA

RETREAT

Light Cavalry

Dragoons

Light Infantry Cos.

71st Foot

7th Foot

Dragoons

Island Creek

Militia

Militia

MORGAN

PICKENS

HOWARD

WASHINGTON

TARLETON

To Chesnee

N

JDD and TPS

= AMERICANS   = BRITISH

When the British infantry stepped into killing range, the front rank of militia opened fire into the massed formations. Just as Morgan had asked of them, they fired two good volleys before easing rearward toward Colonel Pickens's second line. The move disturbed Pickens's formation, which he quickly reformed, augmented with breathless militia from the first line. At about 100 yards Pickens ordered his men to fire into the advancing British infantry. According to most accounts, the British losses at this stage of the battle were severe, especially in officers. Virginia riflemen posted on the flanks cut apart the dragoons and drove them back. With their duty done, the second line of militia scampered off to the left as ordered, though the movement was almost certainly more chaotic than usually portrayed. The 17th Dragoons on Tarleton's right believed the enemy was retreating and galloped forward to cut apart the militia. Washington's cavalry and Virginia riflemen tore them apart and drove the unit rearward in confusion.

Colonel Howard and his Continentals, meanwhile, waited for Tarleton's men in the third and last line of defense. In a repeat performance, the British marched into range and Howard's men greeted them with well delivered volleys. With the Virginia riflemen posted on the flanks, the British were now within a large and effective kill zone—exactly as Morgan had planned. This phase developed into an extended slugfest that Tarleton himself admitted "produced much slaughter." The climax of the battle was at hand.

Tarleton ordered up the Highlanders to crush Morgan's right flank. Howard's order to refuse the right side of his line to meet the attack resulted in some confusion, but when his men steadied themselves and fired into the advancing Highlanders at close range, Howard sensed the enemy was wavering. He ordered his men to follow it up with a charge with fixed bayonets. In conjunction with Washington's cavalry, Howard's assaulting troops surprised the British. Most turned and fled, but many threw down their arms and asked for quarter. Within a few minutes the retreat on Tarleton's left turned into a complete rout. The long night, poor rations, and rigorous fighting had drained away any British will to continue the combat.

In one last desperate effort to save the day, Tarleton ordered his own cavalry command to charge the American riflemen. Exhausted and ill-disciplined, the 200 or so dragoons refused and rode off the field. With perhaps 55 riders Tarleton launched a forlorn hope. Washington's troopers countercharged and a short brutal fight was waged, the saber-wielding horsemen slashing at one another. Although it only lasted for a few minutes, the action was one of the most dramatic cavalry fights of the war.

With his army fleeing the field (the collapse was so sudden the pair of field pieces were abandoned) Tarleton had no choice but to admit defeat. His command had been nearly wiped out. Washington's cavalry pursued the beaten enemy for much of the day. With Cornwallis's command just 20 miles away and closing, Morgan paroled captive British officers, entrusted the wounded to the care of the locals, and retreated northward with his victorious—and elated—army.

Casualties: British: 110 killed, 200 wounded, and 529 captured; American: 12 killed and 60 wounded.

Outcome / Impact: Morgan's tremendous victory was achieved against one of the most notorious (though grudgingly respected) British officers. Rifle fire had picked apart the British officer corps, killing 39 and wounding 27. In addition to winning the field, Morgan's men captured 100 horses, 70 slaves, two sets of the King's colors, 800 muskets, two light field pieces, 35 wagons, and a large quantity of badly needed supplies. Immediately after the battle Morgan led his men safely into North Carolina, where he joined forces with General Greene to plot how best to defeat Cornwallis.

The victory raised the morale of American soldiers in every theater of war. Colonel Andrew Pickens was promoted to brigadier general, and Lieutenant Colonel Washington was awarded a Congressional Gold Medal for his outstanding tactical handling of the cavalry. Despite his stunning success, advanced age, fever, arthritis, and stress finally caught up with old Dan Morgan. The rugged frontiersman retired from active service.

The defeat angered Cornwallis. Not only did it revive enemy morale, but it effectively eviscerated his army's fast and light striking force (Tarleton). Leaving Lord Rawdon to defend South Carolina, Cornwallis pursued Morgan in an effort to destroy him. The frigid temperatures and rain-swollen rivers, however, prevented Cornwallis and his slow-moving army from catching up with Morgan, who marched quickly north across the Catawba River. Infuriated but committed to his policy of invading North Carolina, Cornwallis destroyed his wagon train and excess baggage in an effort to turn his army into a more mobile force to catch Morgan and Greene. The eventual result would be the combat at Guilford Courthouse on March 15, 1781.

Further Reading: Babits, Lawrence, *A Devil of a Whipping: The Battle of Cowpens* (Chapel Hill, 1998); Bearss, Edwin C., *The Battle of Cowpens* (Washington, D.C., 1967); Buchanan, John, *The Road to Guilford Courthouse: The American Revolution in the Carolinas* (John Wiley and Sons, 1999); Lumpkin,

Henry, *From Savannah to Yorktown: The American Revolution in the South* (Paragon House, 1981); Tarleton, Banastre, *A History of the Campaigns of 1780 and 1781, in the Southern Provinces of North America* (Cadell, 1787).

Pensacola, Siege of (Spanish Campaign)

Date: March 9 – May 10, 1781.
Region: Spanish Territory (West Florida)
Commanders: British: Major General John Campbell; Spanish: Field Marshal Bernardo de Gálvez; French: Claude Anne, Marquis de St. Simon
Time of Day / Length of Action: Two-month siege
Weather Conditions: Warm, unremarkable
Opposing Forces: British: 1,600 (two ships); Spanish: 7,025 (64 ships); French: 725 (8 ships)

British Perspective: In January 1779, Maj. Gen. John Campbell waded ashore at Pensacola in the West Florida Territory (today's Florida) with a column from Jamaica. His 1,200-man composite force of British Regulars, Hessian Waldeckers, and Loyalist (Provincial) militiamen bolstered the 1,500-man British defense force assigned to a territory extending from Pensacola in the east to the Mississippi River fortifications in the west. At that time, Pensacola was a small coastal town with roughly 400 citizens and a small garrison of troops who occupied a log and sand palisade protecting the port. Shortly after their arrival Spain entered the war as an American ally. Its entry prompted the British to improve their fortifications to better defend the region from Spanish aggression.

The Crown also maintained small garrisons and forts at Mobile (Alabama), Natchez (Mississippi), and Baton Rouge (Louisiana). The British alliance with the local Choctaw Indians was used to wage small engagements against Spanish troops in Louisiana and Florida. In 1780, the strategic situation changed when Spain organized a campaign to eliminate the British presence in West Florida. Campbell's troops notwithstanding, the Spanish dominated the fighting and in May and June of that year laid siege to British outposts across the region. The British garrison at Mobile surrendered in May; a six-week siege of Fort Panmure at Natchez resulted in the surrender of that place on June 22, 1780. General Campbell had sent reinforcements, but they did not reach the outposts in time to save them.

Certain that Pensacola was the next target on the Spanish wish list, Campbell bolstered the port's defenses at Fort George and at Red Cliffs (now known as Fort Barrancas at the entrance to the bay). He also raised reinforcements with assistance from the local Creek Indians, which increased the British defense force to nearly 2,000 men. The British had several warships in the bay defending the port city, but if the Spanish managed to slip a larger fleet past them and the Royal Navy redoubt gun emplacements at Red Cliffs, the city was doomed. Campbell knew he would be fighting alone, for there were no reinforcements available. The entry of France and now Spain in the American rebellion spread the Crown's resources dangerously thin.

At 8:00 a.m. on March 9, 1781, HMS *Mentor* fired her signal guns: the enemy fleet had sailed into sight. The Spanish fleet approaching Pensacola from the southern end of the bay was huge (38 warships in the initial wave), and prompted Campbell to send HMS *Childers* to Jamaica to seek reinforcements. The Spanish commander deployed troops onto neighboring Santa Rosa Island before sailing his fleet under the guns of the British Royal Navy Redoubt at Red Cliffs. Within a few hours Pensacola Bay was filled with Spanish warships. On the 24th of March, the fleet sailed north and launched an amphibious assault with small water craft to secure a position within Sutton's Lagoon. The beachhead was just two miles west of Fort George, a four-sided fortification well armed with artillery. Two main strongholds, Prince of Wales Redoubt and the Queen's Redoubt, guarded the approaches to the garrison.

On March 25, Campbell ordered a series of probing assaults against the Spanish. The probes gleaned but little information at the cost of a few casualties, and Campbell withdrew the men into the fort. During the next few weeks the Spanish continued landing troops and equipment, assembling a large assault column while the British looked on helplessly, their options limited to their resources on hand.

Spanish-Allied Perspective: Early in the American Revolution, the Spanish government provided covert aid to the Americans in the form of loans and war materiel. Once they formally allied themselves with the French and Americans in May of 1779, however, the Spanish aggressively fought the British for control of the Caribbean Isles, Louisiana, the Mississippi River Valley, and West Florida. Led by Governor Bernardo de Gálvez, the Spanish territorial authority based in New Orleans, the Spanish army prepared to make war against the British in a military campaign labeled by some historians as "Washington's second front."

Governor Gálvez was an effective 33-year-old leader who used his keen intellect and influence with local Indians to great advantage. Gálvez mobilized both local militias and regular Spanish forces for a campaign to eliminate the British threat in the region. By attacking isolated British outposts and shipping with overwhelming forces, the Spanish quickly dominated the Mississippi River Valley. By October 1779, they secured Natchez (present-day Mississippi) and Baton Rouge (present-day Louisiana). In May 1780, they defeated the British at Mobile (present-day Alabama). That June, the Spanish were forced into another battle at Natchez, which ended in their favor after a six-week siege. The British unsuccessfully attempted to retake Mobile in 1781, but the Spanish repulsed them. With the British defeated in the west, Gálvez focused on Pensacola. The King of Spain promoted Gálvez to field marshal and extended his command to include the entire territory. After establishing a strong presence at each of the former British garrisons in the Mississippi delta, Gálvez sailed to Cuba to prepare for the Pensacola operation.

In Havana, Gálvez took control of an armada that included thousands of Spanish infantry, his Louisiana militia, and dozens of Spanish warships to carry them across the gulf to attack Pensacola. Gálvez's army included elements of the King, Crown, Prince, Sorio, Mallorca, Guadalajara, Aragon, Cataluna, Navarra, Toledo, Louisiana, and Hibernia regiments, as well as the Royal Corps of Artillery and a contingent of naval marines. His thrust into the underbelly of England's American presence assisted America's struggle for independence by siphoning off British assets that could have otherwise been employed elsewhere.

After early attempts to deploy were hampered by hurricanes, the persistent Spaniards arrived off the coast of Santa Rosa Island on March 9, 1781. Slipping under the guns at Red Cliffs, which guarded the bay's entry to the Bay of Pensacola, the Spaniards landed on the mainland southwest of Pensacola and secured a base of operations there. The withdrawal of British ships provided freedom of movement for the Spanish fleet. By March 24, Gálvez outnumbered his enemy three to one on land and his vast fleet of ships dominated the bay.

Beginning on March 25, the British launched small hit and run assaults that did little other than irritate Gálvez's men, though Creek Indian forays behind the lines unnerved some of the Spanish troops. On April 19, 1,600 additional Spanish troops arrived, and three days later French troops commanded by Marquis de St. Simon reached Pensacola Bay. St. Simon had with him four frigates and four transport ships containing 725 additional troops. These French regiments had been stationed in nearby Haiti and Santo Domingo, and included the following regiments: Poitiou, Agénois, Orléans, Gâtinois, Cambrésis, Regiment le Cap, the Chasseur Company, and the Royal Corps of Artillery. Gálvez now had a combined force of 7,800 soldiers and several thousand seamen aboard 68 warships.

Gálvez's plan was to extend his position north and build a trench line running eastward onto higher ground around and behind Fort George. From this location he could employ artillery from dominant ground above the fort and bombard the British into submission.

Terrain: Today, Pensacola is a modern metropolitan center and a gulf coast beach resort city. In 1781, it was a small coastal port town. Pensacola is located in the northwest Panhandle region of Florida. Its beaches are sandy and the terrain is generally flat with marshy swamps along the inlets. The town is shielded from the Gulf of Mexico by narrow sandbars and Santa Rosa Island, a natural barrier island to the south. The Bay of Pensacola was about 30 feet deep in 1781, and the water over the bar measured 21 feet. Entrance to the bay was gained through a narrow passage southwest of Pensacola between Perdido Key to the west and Santa Rosa Island to the east. Ships moving into the bay had to run along a narrow strip of land at Red Cliffs (now known as Fort Barrancas and Pensacola Naval Air Station), with the bay opening wide to the north and east once past that point. Once inside, the bay measures six miles north to south (Pensacola to Santa Rosa Island) and six miles from east to west (from Gulf Breeze to Red Cliffs). Although the bay was even larger to the north and east, the room to maneuver available during the siege of Pensacola was restricted to the area described above.

The Spanish mainland assault point at Bayou Chico (then known as Sutton's Lagoon) was two miles southwest of Fort George. The elevation above sea level at Fort George is 32 feet, the ground comprised of sandy soil. In 1781, Pensacola was restricted to the southern coast and Fort George was located north of it, about 1,000 yards inland.

The Fighting: Gálvez's men slowly dug a deep trench and dragged their field pieces through it onto new positions on the high ground. When the Spanish succeeded in placing a battery of six 24-pounders on this forward position, the British wasted no time attacking it. On May 1, from a redoubt between Fort George and the Spanish, British infantry assaulted Gálvez's

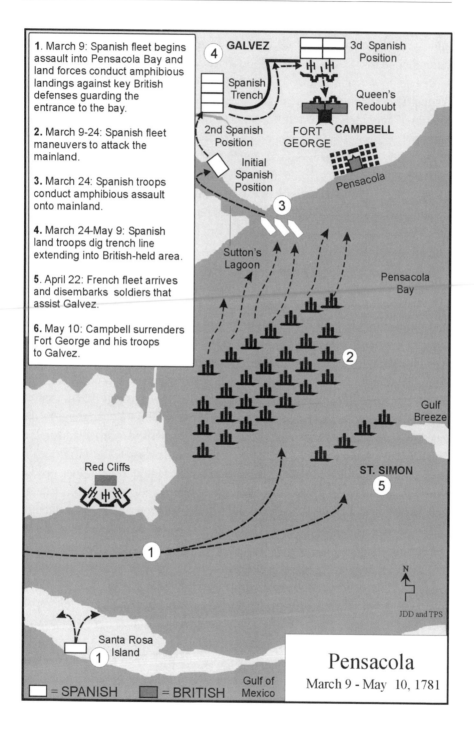

1. March 9: Spanish fleet begins assault into Pensacola Bay and land forces conduct amphibious landings against key British defenses guarding the entrance to the bay.

2. March 9-24: Spanish fleet maneuvers to attack the mainland.

3. March 24: Spanish troops conduct amphibious assault onto mainland.

4. March 24-May 9: Spanish land troops dig trench line extending into British-held area.

5. April 22: French fleet arrives and disembarks soldiers that assist Galvez.

6. May 10: Campbell surrenders Fort George and his troops to Galvez.

GALVEZ

3d Spanish Position

Spanish Trench

Queen's Redoubt

2nd Spanish Position

FORT GEORGE

CAMPBELL

Initial Spanish Position

Pensacola

Sutton's Lagoon

Pensacola Bay

Gulf Breeze

Red Cliffs

ST. SIMON

N

JDD and TPS

Santa Rosa Island

□ = SPANISH   ▨ = BRITISH

Gulf of Mexico

Pensacola

March 9 - May 10, 1781

advance positions. The fighting was sharp and killed and wounded dozens of men. Among the Spanish wounded was Field Marshal Gálvez, who suffered from injuries to his abdomen and hand.

Artillery duels occupied the next several days. On May 6, a combined force made up of the Hessian 3rd Waldeck Regiment and Provincial Tory Loyalists from Pennsylvania and Maryland assaulted the Spanish trenches with fixed bayonets. The attack caught the Spaniards off guard, their arms stacked while their owners ate lunch. Although they suffered dozens of casualties, the Spanish drove the British again. Two days later a Spanish artillery round scored a direct hit into a powder magazine dug into one of the forward British positions. The massive explosion killed and wounded scores of men and opened a gaping hole in General Campbell's defenses, through which Spanish infantry poured. The stunned British survivors retreated to Fort George or fled the scene of carnage as deserters. The Spaniards, meanwhile, rolled their artillery forward as fast as possible and began firing south into Fort George. The direct close range fire sealed Campbell's fate. Unable to shield his men from the bombardment, without the hope of reinforcements, and unable to retreat, Campbell raised a surrender flag at 3:00 p.m. on May 9. A formal surrender was concluded the following day.

Casualties: British: 105 men were reported killed and wounded (Indian losses unknown), 1,113 were captured and sent to New York as prisoners, and 300 men were paroled to Georgia; Spanish: 74 killed and 198 wounded.

Outcome / Impact: The multi-national Allied effort at Pensacola was eerily similar to what General Cornwallis was about to face in Virginia at Yorktown. In both instances control of the seas, coupled with a traditional siege on land, cut off defending British armies and forced their surrender. In both cases the British attempted traditional small-scale assault tactics, to no avail. After the victory Gálvez provided his French reinforcements with 100,000 pesos and urged them on to Virginia, where they joined the French fleet and participated in the naval blockade and siege of Yorktown.

Strategically, the siege of Pensacola played a minor (though notable and largely overlooked) role in America's struggle to cast Great Britain out of North America. The major campaign tied down precious British resources, forced the Crown to cast anxious eyes about much of the globe, and freed French troops to assist General Washington in Virginia. The British could not afford to dispatch any troops from the Caribbean or East Florida to west Florida for fear of the powerful Spanish presence.

Gálvez sealed his string of astounding victories by securing his stronghold at Pensacola, across West Florida and the Mississippi River Valley, and in the Caribbean. When he returned to Spain, King Carlos III promoted him to the rank of lieutenant general, made him the governor of West Florida and Louisiana, and bestowed several titles upon him, including Count of Gálvez and Viscount of Galveztown. Gálvez's victories during the American Revolution (and more direct Spanish aid as well) resulted in Spain being awarded both East and West Florida in the 1783 Treaty of Paris.

Because of the assistance rendered by the Spanish forces to the American cause of liberty, descendants of Hispanic troops who served in North America are eligible for membership in the Sons of the American Revolution and the Daughters of the American Revolution.

Further Reading: Caughey, John Walton, *Bernardo de Gálvez in Louisiana 1776-1783* (University of California Press, 1934); Lang, James, *Conquest and Commerce Spain and England in the Americas* (Academic Press, 1975); Langley, Lester D., *Struggle for the American Mediterranean: United States-European Rivalry in the Gulf-Caribbean, 1776-1904* (University of Georgia Press, 1969); McDermott, John Francis, ed., *The Spanish in the Mississippi Valley, 1762-1804* (University of Illinois Press, 1974); Thomson, Buchannon Parker, *Spain: Forgotten Ally of the American Revolution* (The Christopher Publishing House, 1976).

Yorktown, Siege of (Yorktown Campaign)

Date: September 28 – October 18, 1781

Region: Southern Colonies, Virginia

Commanders: British: Lieutenant General Charles Cornwallis, Brigadier General Charles O'Hara, and Lieutenant Colonels Banastre Tarleton and Robert Abercrombie; Hessians: Colonel F.A.V. Voit von Salzburg and Lieutenant Colonel de Deybothen; American: General George Washington, Major General Benjamin Lincoln, and Major Generals Marquis Maria de Lafayette and Baron Frederich Wilhelm von Steuben; French: Lieutenant Generals le Counts Francois Joseph Paul de Grasse and Jean de Vimeur de Rochambeau, and Comte Claude Gabriel de Choisey

Time of Day / Length of Action: 21-day siege

Weather Conditions: Mild and generally unremarkable fall weather

Opposing Forces: British: 8,000 (soldiers and sailors); Franco-American: 16,645 (American: 8,845; French: 7,800)

British Perspective: After his exhausting campaign in the Carolinas and his bloody tactical "victory" at Guilford Courthouse in March 1781, Lt. Gen. Charles Cornwallis refitted his army in Wilmington, North Carolina, and marched north into Virginia, believing decisive victory was more likely there. He reached Williamsburg in late June and after a flurry of contradictory and confusing orders from his superior, Gen. Sir Henry Clinton, began establishing a base on the York River in August. His main position was in and around Yorktown, Virginia, a small prosperous city of several hundred houses and an important inland port with strategic value to the British. The key to holding Yorktown rested with the British navy. On September 5 at the Battle of the Capes, however, French warships severely damaged a British fleet and blocked England's access to the Chesapeake. With a Franco-American army now blocking a move inland, Cornwallis's position at Yorktown began to assume the look of a self-imposed trap.

Cornwallis set his army to improving its defensive line of works around Yorktown, which were wholly unready to stand a serious siege. Gloucester Point on the north side of the York River was also fortified. On September 28, the combined Franco-American army left Williamsburg and arrived outside Yorktown.

With 7,200 men, including a large contingent of Hessian troops, Cornwallis established a strong inner line of entrenchments around Yorktown supported by detached redoubts and other fortifications in an outer ring of defenses. The outer line encircled the main line from Yorktown Creek in the west and southwest all the way around to the south and back to Wormley's Creek and Pond in the east and southeast. The creeks were deep natural obstacles with marshy banks that wound their way around Yorktown and emptied to the north in the York River. Four redoubts were placed along the outer line in the south, but they were primarily to guard the roads leading into town and were not connected to the inner line of trenches. To the northwest, where the Williamsburg Road crossed Yorktown Creek, was a large and strong star-shaped redoubt. The fortification blocked access to Yorktown along the main road, with the river immediately behind it. It was manned primarily by the 23rd Regiment ("Royal Welch Fusiliers") and often referred to as the "Fusiliers' Redoubt." Cornwallis's troops had cleared deep fields of fire around and beyond the detached works to assist the artillery and the aim of small arms fire against an approaching enemy. The inner line was much stronger and contained interconnecting trenches, redoubts, and batteries. Cornwallis had 65 field pieces, including several 18-pounders removed from the British ships anchored off Yorktown.

North of Yorktown on the other side of the York River was the small town of Gloucester on a spit of land called Gloucester Point. A fortified line to defend the area from a northerly assault was established. It consisted of a single trench line with four redoubts and three batteries, and ran from east to west across the narrow base of the peninsula. Colonel Banastre Tarleton and 700 men from his British Legion manned this line. In addition to the army, Cornwallis also had 800 sailors and a dozen naval vessels that had been trapped in the York River by the French sea victory. The frigates *Charon* and *Guadaloupe*, assisted by supply ships and a few transports, were available to assist in Cornwallis's defense, but their ability to move was restricted.

With little or no access to the sea Cornwallis could not be reinforced, re-supplied, or withdrawn. Each day that passed reduced his food and water supply. His thousands of animals needed forage and grain that was available in limited supplies. His men suffered from bad water, rotting food, and a wide assortment of maladies associated with such hardships. Cornwallis remained curiously passive about his predicament, allowing the enemy to encircle him on the land side without attempting to either march or fight his way out. On September 29, the day after the Franco-American army arrived outside Yorktown, Cornwallis received a message from Gen. Clinton promising reinforcements and the return of the British fleet to assist him. This news convinced Cornwallis he could hold out at Yorktown until reinforcements arrived. Unfortunately for the British, it also convinced him to abandon much of his outer line and concentrate his troops within the inner fortifications. It was a decision that would haunt Cornwallis for the rest of his life.

Franco-American Perspective: George Washington, who was operating in New York, believed Cornwallis's move into Virginia was a strategic mistake. When he learned on August 14 that French Admiral de Grasse's fleet and marines were available until the middle of October, Washington decided on a bold plan. He feinted against New York to confuse General Clinton and stole a march south into Virginia. Bolstered by Comte de Rochambeau's French troops, who had arrived in the colonies in the summer of 1780, Washington moved his army into Williamsburg on September 14, blocking Cornwallis's ready access inland. The French naval victory off the Capes blocked British access to the bay and Cornwallis, while guaranteeing Washington that French artillery and siege equipment could be landed.

With his enemy trapped at Yorktown, Washington and his French allies moved swiftly to establish a traditional siege. On September 17, Washington and Rochambeau met with de Grasse aboard his flagship *La Ville de Paris* to coordinate the joint operation. Washington was assured the French would remain in position until at least October 31. On September 28, the siege of Yorktown was officially begun with French warships blocking the Chesapeake Bay and the Franco-American army positioned outside the British fortifications.

The Allied army was organized into three divisions. Rochambeau commanded the French contingent of about 7,800 men. They occupied the left wing (or northwestern sector) of the siege line. Rochambeau's army consisted of three infantry brigades, a heavy cavalry corps, and a large artillery corps. Duke Armand Louis de Lauzun led the cavalry and Col. François-Marie d'Aboville commanded the artillery. The right or southern sector of the siege line formed the base of the two wings boasting 8,845 American troops. These were divided into three divisions led by Major General Lincoln (commanding the American wing and his own division), and Maj. Gens. Lafayette and von Steuben. Colonel Henry Knox was in charge of the American artillery, engineers, sappers, and miners, and Col. Stephen Moylan led the cavalry. The third division of the Allied army was comprised of 3,200 Virginia militiamen. It occupied the southeastern sector or far right wing of the siege line. Brigadier General Thomas Nelson, Jr., commanded these men; his unit commanders were Brig. Gens. George Weedon, Edward Stevens, and Robert Lawson.

The Franco-American siege line was initially established two miles below Yorktown in a giant arc, with the French on the west (left) and the Americans in the south (center) and east (right). Additionally, Washington dispatched four regiments led by Comte Claude Gabriel de Choisey to the northern side of the York River to lay siege to the British troops operating on Gloucester Point. There, 1,500 Virginia militiamen commanded by Brig. Gen. George Weedon, aided by 1,400 French troops under Duke de Lauzun, joined forces to bottle up the enemy.

Terrain: Located in the Tidewater region of Virginia, Yorktown rests on the northern border of a large peninsula formed by the James River on the south and the York River on the north. Yorktown is on the southern shore of the York River, and Gloucester Point is on the opposite bank. Both positions are 35 miles inland, northwest of Cape Henry, and 15 miles east of Williamsburg. Yorktown was a natural inland port, with access to both the sea lanes to the east and Williamsburg and other points inland. It was thus an important trans-shipment hub for the state of Virginia. The river between the British defenses at Yorktown and Gloucester Point was about three-quarters of a mile wide. Gloucester Point extends from north to south into the York River, which made it an ideal location to guard the port from a land assault in the north.

The land around Yorktown is generally flat with some undulation. In 1781, the countryside was cultivated with corn, tobacco, and grains to the south, while the land west and east of the city was cut by meandering creeks, ravines, and dense patches of woods. Four main roads served Yorktown in 1781, two to the north and west and two to the south and east. The water above and below the town anchored Cornwallis's defenses.

The Fighting: During the first few days of the siege, skirmishing occurred at various points along the line as the troops began establishing patrols and organizing their assigned sectors. On September 29, the Americans in the eastern sector (right wing) began reconnoitering the area and a minor skirmish broke out at Wormley Creek. The British simply fell back to their trenches and the Americans broke contact.

On September 30, a heavier skirmish west of the Fusiliers' Redoubt between the British and French forces resulted in several casualties. To the surprise of the Allies, on that same day the British evacuated most of their outer works, which French and Americans happily and quickly occupied. On October 3, the small but fascinating Battle of the Hook was fought north of Gloucester Point when Colonel Tarleton and a detachment of dragoons guarding foraging wagons ran into advancing Allied forces. The brisk fight began when Lauzon's French cavalry attacked the British. Tarleton was knocked from his horse and nearly killed or captured, only to be saved by his men at the last moment. American militia arrived and boldly stood in the face of a charge. British infantry was also lightly involved. Tarleton wisely retreated within the defensive lines on Gloucester Point. Casualty figures vary widely. Allied losses were about five killed and 27 wounded. British losses were about 50 killed and wounded. It was the last battle the despised Tarleton would fight in the American Revolution.

The construction of the first Allied parallel or siege line began during the first week of October. The line was laid out in a concave arc from west of Hampton Road in the French sector east and then northeast into the American sector, anchored at each end by, respectively, the Grand French Battery Complex and the American Grand Battery. The line was about

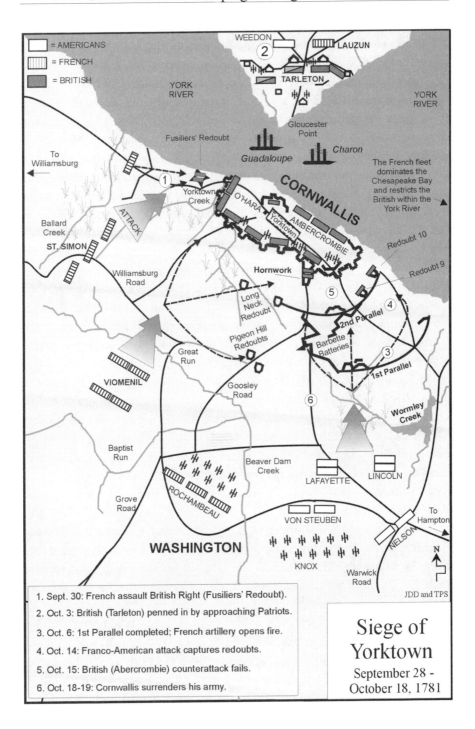

1. Sept. 30: French assault British Right (Fusiliers' Redoubt).
2. Oct. 3: British (Tarleton) penned in by approaching Patriots.
3. Oct. 6: 1st Parallel completed; French artillery opens fire.
4. Oct. 14: Franco-American attack captures redoubts.
5. Oct. 15: British (Abercrombie) counterattack fails.
6. Oct. 18-19: Cornwallis surrenders his army.

JDD and TPS

Siege of Yorktown
September 28 -
October 18, 1781

800-1,000 yards from the main line of British works and roughly the same one evacuated by the British. Allied troops worked night and day on the construction of gabions (large woven baskets filled with earth) to bolster the trenches, fascines (bundled timbers), fraises (sharpened stakes directed at the enemy), and saucissons (large sharpened logs pointed at the enemy) to improve their lines. The British ineffectually bombarded the Allies with artillery fire during its construction. On the night of October 6, a French diversion on the left toward the Fusiliers' Redoubt helped focus attention on that distant flank and away from the digging of the first parallel. Once the line was finished and artillery was emplaced, the Allies opened a relentless bombardment against British positions. The fire inflicted scores of casualties and sank, burned, or drove off several ships anchored off Yorktown.

It was now time to dig a second siege line to further strangle Cornwallis's defenders. The line was begun on October 11 and spotted by Cornwallis at dawn the following morning. This line, about 750 yards long, was within musket and easy artillery range of the British main line. The British response drove the workers to ground and brought work, temporarily, to a halt. On the east or right wing sector of the field work was made doubly difficult by the presence of two strong British forts: Redoubts 9 and 10. Both were well defended and blocked the extension of the siege line in that direction. Washington decided to assault and capture the strongholds. The French were ordered to conduct a feint in the western sector against the Fusiliers' Redoubt to distract the enemy, while a simultaneous action was conducted at Gloucester Point. Under cover of darkness on October 14, meanwhile, two columns (one French and one American) would attack Redoubts 9 and 10, respectively.

At 8:00 p.m., 400 Americans led by Col. Alexander Hamilton stormed Redoubt 10, the fort closest to the York River. The Continentals climbed up, over, and through the British fraises, abatis, and saucissons ringing the redoubt. The fight only lasted about 10 minutes before the Americans were in possession of it. American losses were nine dead and 25 wounded; British casualties were about eight killed and wounded and 20 captured, the rest escaping back to the main line. On Hamilton's left was the 400-man French column under Col. William Deux Ponts. These men attacked and captured British Redoubt Number 9. Their losses were heavier with 15 killed and 77 wounded. British losses were 18 killed and as many as 50 captured.

That night the Allies began incorporating the forts into the right wing of the second parallel. The batteries could fire and hit any point within

Yorktown. A massed Allied infantry column, at a distance of only 400 or so yards, threatened to penetrate the British lines. Unless Cornwallis did something quickly to turn the tide of the siege, the end was in sight. Before dawn on October 16, 350 British troops commanded by Lt. Col. Robert Abercrombie attacked the center of the American line. The British captured several dozen Americans and spiked a few cannon, but were not strong enough to do more than that before being driven back to their lines. That feeble attempt was all Cornwallis could muster.

That same night Cornwallis ordered the evacuation of his troops to Gloucester Point, but bad weather, a lack of adequate transports, and the Allied bombardment forced him to abort the effort. Cornwallis had decided to attempt a breakthrough and a march northward to New York, but it was simply too little, too late. On October 17, Cornwallis opened surrender negotiations that eventually led to the capitulation of his entire army.

Casualties: British: 156 killed, 326 wounded, and 7,157 prisoners; Franco-American: 274 casualties (French: 52 killed and 134 wounded; American: 23 killed and 65 wounded).

Outcome / Impact: On October 19, 1781, at 2:00 p.m., the British and Hessian defenders of Yorktown officially surrendered. About 2,000 of the surrendered troops were sick or wounded and unable to march. However, 7,157 soldiers, 840 sailors, and 80 camp followers walked out of Yorktown, passing between the French and American soldiers lining the Yorktown-Hampton Road. General Cornwallis claimed he was ill, so Brig. Gen. Charles O'Hara led the surrendered in his absence. The British officers were allowed to keep their side arms, papers, and property, and select officers (including Cornwallis) were given their freedom on parole. However, the British soldiers and sailors were sentenced as prisoners of war to camps in Virginia and Pennsylvania.

Cornwallis boarded the sloop *Bonetta* and sailed to New York, where he officially informed General Clinton of the surrender at Yorktown. When the British fleet carrying the reinforcements Cornwallis so badly needed learned of his capitulation, it returned to New York. Admiral de Grasse returned the French fleet to the West Indies, and the Americans began their return march to the Hudson Highlands of New York on November 1, 1781.

It is impossible to overstate the ramifications of the Allied victory at Yorktown. Without qualification it was the most decisive campaign of the American Revolution. It also demonstrated General Washington's brilliance as a field commander. However, without the assistance of his French allies, the campaign would not have been possible.

British armed forces remained in New York until November 25, 1783, and several minor skirmishes occurred before a final peace was achieved, but the victory at Yorktown assured the end of the war and the beginning of a hard-won peace for a new nation.

Further Reading: Greene, Jerome A., *The Guns of Independence: The Siege of Yorktown, 1781* (Savas Beatie, 2005); Morrissey, Brandon, *Yorktown 1781: The World Turned Upside Down* (Osprey, 1997); Johnston, Henry P., *The Yorktown Campaign and the Surrender of Cornwallis 1781* (Harper & Brothers, 1881).

Illustrations from the Revolution

British Leaders & Their Allies

Sir Henry Clinton (right) fought in North America during the entire war from Bunker Hill through the surrender at Yorktown. From 1778, he served as the British commander-in-chief. *National Park Service, Colonial National Historical Park, Yorktown Collection*

Lieutenant General Charles Cornwallis (left) was one of England's best tactical field commanders. He fought in numerous battles before surrendering his army at Yorktown in 1781. *National Archives*

General Sir William Howe (right) led British forces at Bunker Hill in 1775 and served as commander-in-chief in North America until he resigned in 1778 after the war turned against England. *National Archives*

General Sir Guy Carleton (left) served as Governor of Quebec. He defended the city in late 1775 and led British forces in the Battle of Valcour Island against Benedict Arnold on Lake Champlain in 1776. He was appointed Commander-in-Chief, North America, after Yorktown. *Library of Congress*

General Thomas Gage (right) served in North America from 1763 to 1775. His raids into the Massachusetts countryside to seize gunpowder helped trigger the outbreak of war in April 1775 at Lexington and Concord. He was replaced by General Howe in the fall of 1775 after failing to end the siege of Boston. *National Archives*

General John Burgoyne (left) served in North America from the beginning of the war, but his name will forever be associated with the crippling loss of his entire army in upstate New York in the 1777 Saratoga Campaign. The stunning American victory helped convince France to openly support the war for independence against England. *Independence National Historical Park Collection*

Lieutenant Colonel Banastre Tarleton (left) was a light cavalry commander best known for possible atrocities committed by his men against American troops at the battle of Waxhaws in 1780, and for his crushing defeat at Cowpens in 1781 that nearly destroyed his command. *National Park Service, Colonial National Historical Park, Yorktown Collection*

Major John Pitcairn (top right) was a British marine who led his men up the hill in one of the attacks at Bunker Hill in June 1775. He was mortally wounded by a musket ball and fell into his son's arms, who cried out, "I have lost my father!" *Library of Congress.* **Chief Joseph Brant** (right) was a Mohawk military and political leader. He motivated many Indians to support British efforts and fought in several major battles. *National Archives*

Major General Baron von Riedesel (left) led a Hessian regiment and all German and American Indian forces during the 1777 Saratoga Campaign. He was captured when the British army surrendered. *New York Public Library*

The Americans & Their Allies

When **George Washington** (left) was appointed commander-in-chief in 1775, he had no experience leading an army. His powerful presence, determination, and strong character, however, coupled with his ability to learn from his errors and those of his enemy, bore fruit as the war progressed. His early mistakes (especially on Long Island) nearly ended the bid for independence, but his bold offensives at Trenton and Princeton, followed by a long pitched battle and tactical victory at Monmouth, stabilized the North. Although he had lost earlier at Brandywine and Germantown, Washington understood how and when to fight. In 1781, his sweeping strategic movement south from New York to Virginia trapped General Cornwallis's army at Yorktown. The decisive victory ended military operations in America. *Independence National Historical Park Collection*

General Nathanael Greene (right) began the war as a private and ended it as a major general with a reputation as one of the finest field commanders on either side. He fought in many early battles in the North, including Trenton, Brandywine, and Germantown. At Valley Forge during the difficult spring of 1778, Greene accepted the thankless position of quartermaster general, but still led troops at Monmouth and in the Rhode Island expedition. In 1780, Washington put Greene in charge of the defeated army in the South. His strategic retreat exhausted Cornwallis's British army, which won a tactical victory over Greene at Guilford Courthouse. The crippled Cornwallis, however, ended his Southern operations and moved toward Virginia, and was later defeated at Yorktown.

Independence National Historical Park Collection

General Horatio Gates (right) was commissioned in 1775 as a brigadier general and adjutant. He was one of the few American officers with long experience in the British army. His excellent staff work organizing the early Continental Army is overshadowed by his backdoor efforts to wrest command of the army away from General Washington. In the Northern Department in 1777, Gates's army defeated the British at Saratoga, though historians debate whether he or his subordinates, who led the fighting, deserve most of the credit. In the Southern Department, Gates's army was routed from the field at Camden. *Independence National Historical Park Collection*

Marie Jean Paul Roch Yves Gilbert Motier, Marquis de Lafayette (left) arrived from France in 1777 and joined Washington's staff. He was later given a field command, and led his troops well in the operations leading up to Yorktown, where his men participated in the capture of Redoubt 10. *Independence National Historical Park Collection*

General Benedict Arnold (right) was a capable leader who helped capture Fort Ticonderoga, led a difficult campaign that failed to capture Quebec City, and built a fleet on Lake Champlain which, though defeated at Valcour Island in 1777, delayed the British invasion of New York. That, plus his pivotal role at Saratoga that fall, helped defeat the enemy and turn the tide of war. In 1780, he offered to turn over West Point to the British. He deserted when his plan was discovered, and later led a British army on American soil at New London, Connecticut. *Independence National Historical Park Collection*

General Benjamin Lincoln (right) led troops at Boston, White Plains, and Fort Independence. He played a prominent role in the important victory at Saratoga, where his ankle was badly fractured by enemy fire. When he recovered, he was appointed in 1778 to command the Southern Department. He surrendered Charleston to Sir Henry Clinton in the worst American defeat of the war. Paroled, Lincoln played a prominent role at Yorktown and accepted the sword of surrender there. *Independence National Historical Park Collection*

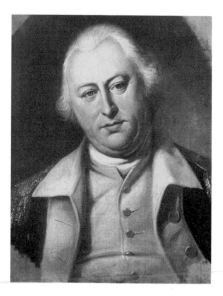

General Henry Knox (left) was present at the Boston Massacre in 1770 and fought at Bunker Hill. He impressed Washington, who gave him an artillery command. Knox moved the captured guns from Fort Ticonderoga to Boston, supervised Washington's crossing of the Delaware River to attack Trenton, and was promoted to general and chief of artillery. He fought to the end of the war. *Independence National Historical Park Collection*

General Daniel Morgan (right) organized a rifle company early in the war and joined Benedict Arnold in his march and siege of Quebec City, where Morgan was wounded, captured, and exchanged. Promoted to regimental command, he served well during the Saratoga Campaign at the battles of Freeman's Farm and Bemis Heights. In the South, Morgan led an army in the decisive January 1781 tactical victory over Banastre Tarleton at Cowpens. The British defeat weakened Cornwallis's efforts in the South. *Independence National Historical Park Collection*

Colonel Henry Lee (left) was one of the best cavalry commanders on either side during the Revolution. The father of Confederate General Robert E. Lee, "Light Horse Harry" led "Lee's Legion," served as Washington's bodyguard at Germantown, and fought well in many actions, including Paulas Hook, Guilford Courthouse, Camden, Eutaw Springs, and Yorktown. *Independence National Historical Park Collection*

General Anthony Wayne (right) led the 4th Pennsylvania Regiment early in the war, participated in Arnold's failed effort to invade Canada, and later led the Pennsylvania line in several major battles, including Brandywine, Germantown, and Monmouth. His brilliant tactical capture of Stony Point on the Hudson River in 1779 was the highlight of his wartime service. He also fought in Virginia during the Yorktown operations. In 1794, "Mad Anthony" commanded an army against Indians in the decisive victory at the Battle of Fallen Timbers (modern Ohio). *Independence National Historical Park Collection*

Nicknamed the "Carolina Gamecock," **Thomas Sumter** (left) led South Carolina troops during much of the war, eventually achieving the rank of brigadier general. He served entirely in the Southern theater, where his sharp and hard fighting tactics earned him both his nickname and a compliment from General Cornwallis that the South Carolinian was his greatest plague. Sumter's efforts helped drive Cornwallis out of the Carolinas and into Virginia. *Independence National Historical Park Collection*

Andrew Pickens (right) fought Indians before the Revolution, and was a prominent militia commander during the war, rising to the rank of brigadier general. He was captured at Charleston and exchanged, and fought in several major actions including Cowpens, the sieges of Augusta, and Fort Ninety-Six, and Eutaw Springs. *Independence National Historical Park Collection*

French Admiral **Francois Joseph Paul, comte de Grasse** (left) is best known for commanding a fleet at the Battle of the Capes (Chesapeake) in September 1781, turning back reinforcements and supplies intended for Cornwallis' besieged army at Yorktown. The admiral was decisively defeated (and captured) in 1782 by a British fleet at the Battle of the Saintes. *National Park Service, Colonial National Historical Park, Yorktown Collection*

General Jean Baptiste Donatien de Vimeur, comte de Rochambeau (right) was a nobleman who commanded the French Expeditionary Force to support the American effort against the British. Rochambeau's legendary cooperation with General Washington, together with his efforts to coordinate Admiral de Grasse's fleet off the Virginia coast, helped trap Cornwallis at Yorktown. *National Park Service, Colonial National Historical Park, Yorktown Collection*

Battles in Illustrations and Artwork

Buford's Massacre, more commonly known as the Battle of Waxhaws, took place on May 29, 1780, in South Carolina. After the British captured Charleston on May 12, General Cornwallis marched his 2,500-man army inland toward Camden, South Carolina. When he learned that the state's governor, John Rutledge, was escaping into North Carolina with perhaps 400 or more Patriots led by Col. Abraham Buford, Cornwallis dispatched Lt. Col. Banastre Tarleton, who had a well deserved reputation as a capable and zealous officer who pushed his dragoons hard and fast, to catch the column. Tartleton's 275 dragoons and infantry caught up with Buford's column on May 29. When the Americans refused an offer to surrender, Tarleton attacked.

Exactly what happened next will forever be subject to dispute. Some sources claim the British grew angry when they learned Tarleton had been struck down (he had not). The dragoons went to work, cutting and slashing the Patriots with their sabers, wounded and unwounded alike. British infantry added their bayonets to the bloody chaos. The hacking and close-quarter fighting, if as extensive as described, probably lasted about fifteen minutes. Surrender was out of the question as no quarter was offered or accepted. Depending on one's perspective, Waxhaws was either a well-executed tactical British victory or a bloody crime. The British only lost four killed and 14 wounded, but the Americans suffered 113 killed, 150 wounded, and 53 captured. Colonel Buford and about 30 men escaped, as did additional infantry at the head of the column who did not turn and form to fight.

Minutemen Depart to Defend Concord

The fight at **Concord** took place just hours after the opening of the war on Lexington Green on April 19, 1775, outside of Boston, Massachusetts. Despite British efforts to march secretly to Concord (six miles distant) to seize stores of American gunpowder, Bostonians Paul Revere and William Dawes rode to raise the alarm and Patriots formed to meet them.

The raid was under the command of Lt. Col. Frances Smith. At Concord, Capt. Lawrence Parsons led three companies to search homes and farms while three more companies under Capt. Walter Laurie marched to secure the North Bridge. Local militia leader Col. James Barrett led a contingent of men to remove munitions and military stores from his property and conceal them elsewhere.

By this time (about 9:30 a.m.), several hundred militia had gathered on the high ground above the bridge. With fife playing and drums beating, Maj. John Buttrick led a motley group of farmers and merchants toward Laurie's companies defending the span. Laurie ordered his men to fall back to the opposite side of the bridge, where they deployed in a tight in-depth defensive formation that allowed only one of the three companies to fire on the approaching rebels, who continued advancing unaware of the brief fight at Lexington.

When the British opened fire the rebels confidently returned it. The exchange lasted for several minutes and drove the Crown's professional soldiers back in some disorder into Concord. They left three killed and eight wounded behind. The Americans suffered two killed and three wounded and made no real attempt to pursue Laurie or cut off the column of British searching Barrett's farm. Smith led the British out of Concord about noon, knowing that the force of Massachusetts militiamen was growing.

The retreat back to Boston was a disaster for the British, who suffered heavy casualties along much of the way as American Minutemen gathered to shoot and harass them. By the time the march ended, as many as 6,000 colonials had assembled on the outskirts of Boston. The raid cost the British 73 killed, 174 wounded, and 26 missing, while American losses were tabulated at 49 killed, 41 wounded, and five missing. Most of these casualties were suffered during the running battle back toward Boston. Lexington and Concord ("The Shot Heard Round The World") initiated armed hostilities between the British and Americans. The shedding of blood was what many in the colonies were hoping for to raise popular support for an armed revolution.

The decisive three-week **Yorktown Campaign** (Sept. 28 – Oct. 18, 1781) in Virginia ended active military operations. The British army and naval force (about 8,000 men) was under the command of Lt. Gen. Charles Cornwallis, with the joint American and French forces (about 16,500) led by Gen. George Washington.

After his exhausting campaign in the Carolinas and bloody tactical victory at Guilford Courthouse in March 1781, Cornwallis rested his army in Wilmington, North Carolina, and then marched north into Virginia. He believed that a decisive victory was more likely there than in the Carolinas. When he reached Williamsburg in late June, Cornwallis followed orders and began establishing a base of operations on the York River that August. His main position was in and around Yorktown, Virginia, an important inland port with strategic value to the British. He could not hold Yorktown without the British navy, however. The Battle of the Capes against a French fleet that September blocked England's access to the Chesapeake Bay. With a Franco-American army cutting off inland access, Cornwallis could not be reinforced, resupplied, or withdrawn. He and his men (including a strong force of Hessians), were effectively trapped. Although his army prepared strong defensive works around Yorktown, they were not suitable for withstanding a serious siege.

As the days passed, Washington's army erected siege lines and began pressing the British closer to Yorktown. On the night of October 11, two storming columns (one French and one American), attacked and captured a pair of strong enemy redoubts. Artillery could not strike anywhere within the British lines. The most Cornwallis could muster in reply was an unsuccessful dawn attack on October 16 by 350 British troops against the center of the American line. That same night he ordered an evacuation across the river, but bad weather, a lack of transports, and Allied artillery ended the effort. The next day Cornwallis agreed to surrender. Yorktown cost the British 156 killed, 326 wounded, and 7,157 prisoners, while the Franco-American army lost 274 casualties (French: 52 killed and 134 wounded; American: 23 killed and 65 wounded). Cornwallis claimed he was ill, so Brig. Gen. Charles O'Hara represented the British during the surrender ceremony. Benjamin Lincoln accepted his sword (which is represented by the illustration below).

Lincoln accepts General O'Hara's word at Yorktown

The Final Cavalry
Fight at Cowpens

The Battle of Cowpens (January 17, 1781) was fought in South Carolina between British forces led by Col. Banastre Tarleton (1,100 men) and an American army led by Brig. Gen. Daniel Morgan (1,065). When Cornwallis learned in early January that Daniel Morgan was operating in the western part of the state, he dispatched Tarleton to defeat him. The aggressive Tarleton pursued Morgan's men northward toward Cowpens, just a few miles below the North Carolina border. He had pushed his command through most of a long cold night's journey of 12 miles before catching up with Morgan at Cowpens about 6:30 a.m. on January 17.

Morgan decided to fight at Cowpens because the position offered good terrain for the type of battle he intended to wage—even though an impassable river was just five miles behind him. His command consisted of about 1,000 soldiers (533 militiamen from Virginia, Georgia, and both Carolinas, 237 Continentals, 80 cavalrymen, and about 200 independent riflemen; estimates vary from 800 to 1,065). Morgan arranged his men in three lines. The first was composed of 150 unreliable militia riflemen as a skirmish line. Morgan asked that they fire twice and then could retire. The militia would fall back 150 yards to the second line, which was held by 300 militia. Morgan cautioned these men to wait until the British were within easy range, aim at the officers, and then after two shots or "hits" retire around the left flank of the third or final line, where they could reform. That line was held by 450 riflemen (mostly Continentals). This base formation was flanked on both sides by 200 independent Virginia riflemen. William Washington (the general's cousin) and his cavalry were in the rear as a reserve.

Pleased the Americans had decided to stand and fight, Tarleton formed his tired command and ordered his men to charge. Morgan's men fought exactly as he had asked, with the front rank of militia firing into the massed formations before falling back. The second line responded the same way. According to most accounts, the British losses at this stage of the battle were severe, especially in officers. The British had no more luck against the line of Continentals, and an infantry attack in conjunction with Washington's cavalry drove most of the redcoats from the field. A desperate British cavalry attack was too late to save the day. Tarleton lost 110 killed, 200 wounded, and 529 captured, while Morgan suffered just 12 killed and 60 wounded.

The Battle of Princeton, January 3, 1777, in New Jersey followed on the heels of George Washington's stunning victory at Trenton on December 26, 1776. The defense of New Jersey was General Cornwallis's responsibility and, like so many others he believed the American army was all but finished. The defeat of the Hessian force at Trenton angered Cornwallis, who was determined to catch and destroy Washington.

On January 3, Cornwallis left Princeton for Trenton with 6,700 men. He left 1,200 men in Princeton, and a similar force midway between Princeton and Trenton. After marching, deploying, and maneuvering, Cornwallis believed he had Washington trapped between the Assunpink and Delaware rivers. Confident of victory, he bedded down for the night in preparation for a battle of elimination the following day.

That night, however, Washington slipped 4,600 men around Cornwallis's left flank while 400 more remained behind to deceive the enemy. While Washington's column moved against the 1,200-man enemy garrison at Princeton under Col. Charles Mawhood, Gen. Hugh Mercer and 350 American infantry deployed as a blocking force two miles to the southwest on the Post Road. Mawhood, however, marched toward Trenton and met Mercer in a small orchard. Both sides deployed quickly into line and began killing one another at a range of only 50 yards. The British were fresh and alert, but the Patriots had marched all night in freezing temperatures. After one volley Mawhood ordered a bayonet charge. Mercer was fighting on foot after his horse was injured, refused to surrender, and was mortally wounded by at least seven bayonet wounds. Unable to withstand British steel, the militia retreated south toward the Back Road. When Washington arrived, the battle turned in favor of the Americans. The battle cost the British 28 killed, 58 wounded, and 187 missing/captured, while the American lost 23 killed and 20 wounded.

The loss of Mercer was a blow to the army. The wounded Mercer lingered in agony until he died on January 11. Many contemporaries and postwar historians believe Mercer was one of the Patriot army's legitimate rising stars.

The Mortal Wounding of Hugh Mercer at Princeton

Brave Sgt. Jasper

The **Battle of Sullivan's Island** (left) at Charleston, South Carolina, on June 28, 1776, pitted a large British fleet (20 ships) under Maj. Gen. Sir Henry Clinton against Americans defending Fort Sullivan under Col. William Moultrie. The massive British bombardment failed. It did, however, cut down the American flag, which Sgt. William Jasper calmly reattached to a new staff at great personal danger to himself.

The **Battle of Wyoming** (below) was fought on July 3, 1778, in the Wyoming Valley of Pennsylvania between British, Tory, and Indian troops (the latter led by Chief Joseph Brant), and Americans under Cols. Zebulon Butler and Nathan Denison. The raid caught settlers there by surprise, and an ambush trapped the American force. The British allowed the Indians to torture, scalp, and kill their prisoners.

Captives at the Battle of Wyoming

Fighting Indians at Blue Licks

Many engagements during the Revolutionary War included Indians, including the little-known **Battle of Blue Licks** (present-day Kentucky) on August 19, 1782—nearly one year *after* Cornwallis surrendered his army at Yorktown. Several battles in the Ohio Indian lands, including the June 4-5, 1782 fight at Sandusky (also known as the Sandusky Expedition), and Olentangy, which was fought the following day, served as a catalyst for the Blue Licks combat. Hundreds of Americans were killed during these engagements, many tortured and some burned at the stake, and large numbers of Indians, upon whose lands the whites were encroaching, were also killed.

Destroying Indian Villages

Baron von Steuben
Training Troops

Friedrich Wilhelm von Steuben (above) was a Prussian military officer who served as inspector general and as a major general in the Continental Army. His training improved the abilities and morale of American troops. Later in the war, he served as Gen. Washington's chief of staff. Living through winters (below) out in the field was especially hard on American troops. A lack of quality food, warm clothing, and the spread of deadly diseases—as the 1777-1778 experience at Valley Forge came to symbolize—inflicted tremendous suffering.

Wintering in Camp

Native Americans in the American Revolution

Following the end of the French and Indian War, the Proclamation of 1763 (as decreed by King George III of Great Britain) declared that all lands west of the Allegheny Mountains belonged to the Indians. This act forbade settlers from encroaching deeper into what was now recognized as Indian territories. Several aggressive land companies, however, continued their crooked dealings with the Indians. Ultimately, these illegal land transactions, coupled with continuing explorations of the French, British, and Spanish into the unsettled territories, would trigger repeated hostilities with Native Americans.

The close of the French and Indian War left American Indians with little more than open promises, famine, and disease. These unfortunate circumstances were further enflamed in 1774 when Governor John Murray (Lord Dunmore) of Virginia launched a campaign against the Indians in the western region of Pennsylvania, down into the Ohio River Valley, and into the northwestern mountains of Virginia (present-day West Virginia). This armed incursion crossed the Allegheny boundary into what was known as "Indian lands," and resulted in reprisal attacks along the frontier by both the Shawnee and Delaware. The larger Iroquois nation to the north remained out of the fight and a temporary peace treaty was negotiated between the British authority of Indian Affairs, Sir Guy Johnson, and the very influential Iroquois Chief Joseph Bryant.

At the same time, in what is today Kentucky, eastern Tennessee, southwestern Virginia, western South Carolina, and northern Georgia, white settlers continued encroaching into lands belonging to the Cherokee, Catawba, and Creek nations. Mountain men, known as the "Long Hunters," blazed trails deep into Indian territories. These men returned with settlers who established forts and outposts throughout the region. These early settlements were established and defended by such men as Daniel Boone, Lazarus Dameron, and John Sevier. These backwoodsmen served as hunters, guides, Indian fighters (known then as Indian Spies), and early community leaders. Temporary peace accords were achieved between the Indian chiefs of these southern Indian lands and the Indian agent, John Stuart.

In 1775, these temporary peace accords between the Indians and white settlers were turned upside down when the colonists revolted against the Crown. Lieutenant General Thomas Gage, the British authority in North America, ordered his Indian agents to "deliver war upon the colonists" wherever possible, a decision that triggered a wave of bloody violence throughout the settlements and border regions of the Allegheny Mountains. Thomas Jefferson, author of the American Declaration of Independence, blamed King George for endeavoring "to bring on the inhabitants of our frontiers, the merciless Indian savages, whose known rule of warfare is undistinguished destruction of all ages, sexes and conditions."

Spurred on by the British, Indians all along the frontier (except for the Oneida and Tuscarora tribes) went on the warpath against white settlers. During the summer of 1777, the Indians joined with British and Tory forces against the Americans. Fighting intensified all along the frontier. The Iroquois participated in the battles of Oriskany and Fort Stanwix, and Freeman's Farm, all related parts of the larger 1777 Saratoga Campaign in New York. Both sides launched bloody raiding parties along the frontier and, depending upon which side you were on, the event was referred to as a "massacre," further enflaming tensions and hatred. During the next few years the bloodshed intensified in the Wyoming and Ohio Valleys, and especially in the interior of New York in the Cherry and Lackawanna Valley regions.

To counter the deadly Indian raids conducted against settlers in New York, in the summer of 1779, Gen. Washington dispatched General John Sullivan and 4,000 Continental troops with the following mission:

> *The immediate objects are the total destruction and devastation of their settlements, and the capture of as many prisoners of every age and sex as possible. It will be essential to ruin their crops now in the ground and prevent their planting more.*
>
> *I would recommend, that some post in the center of the Indian Country, should be occupied with all expedition, with a sufficient quantity of provisions whence parties should be detached to lay waste all the settlements around, with instructions to do it in the most effectual manner, that the country may not be merely overrun, but destroyed.*
>
> *But you will not by any means listen to any overture of peace before the total ruinment of their settlements is effected.*

Contrary to folklore, early Indians of the eastern forests were not a nomadic people. They eked out villages and towns and planted small crop fields, which made them extremely vulnerable to organized attacks. The resulting "scorched earth" effort conducted by Sullivan's expedition rippled through the Iroquois tribes of the north and nearly destroyed them. The end result was continued bloodshed long after the American Revolution ended. However, Sullivan did succeed in his mission, and at least in the Northern theater of war, the Indian threat was greatly diminished for the remainder of the conflict.

In the Southern theater, meanwhile, the fighting continued along the frontier. Cherokee Chief Dragging Canoe, who promised to turn the ground "dark and bloody," launched deadly raids against settlers in that region. The Watauga and Nolichucky settlements (present-day East Tennessee) and the Clinch River and Holston River settlements of southwest Virginia were particularly isolated and frequently attacked. With nearly 14,000 Cherokee, Choctaws, Creeks, and Chickasaw warriors, the frontier fight with the Indians kept the Southern militiamen busy while the British led by Lord Cornwallis cut a swath through Georgia, the Carolinas, and northward into Virginia (where he would meet his fate at Yorktown).

The Governor of Virginia, Thomas Jefferson, was forced to address the threat in the frontier. "The Cherokees will now be driven beyond the Mississippi and that this in future will be declared to the Indians the invariable consequence of their beginning a war," he announced. "Our contest with Britain is too serious and too great to permit any possibility of avocation from the Indians." In response to Jefferson's call, Gen. Charles Lee, commander of the Southern Continental forces, sent his men into action.

The Southern Indian tribes faced the wrath of the white settlers when Cols. Isaac Shelby and John Sevier led massive raids against their towns in what are today the states of Tennessee, Kentucky, and Georgia. Within a one-year period beginning in December of 1779, the upper, middle, and lower Indian villages were crushed by avenging frontier militias. In retaliatory strikes, the whites wiped out at least 170 villages in their effort to destroy the Indians in that region.

Simultaneously, in the deep South, America's Spanish ally, General Bernardo de Gálvez, attacked British outposts and Indians in the Mississippi Valley, destroying the ability of the Chickasaw, Choctaw, and Creek Indians to assist the Cherokees or to retaliate from that area.

As the American Revolution drew to a close with the Treaty of Paris in 1783, the Indian situation in America was simply ignored. This mistake returned to haunt the newly created United States. As far as the Americans were concerned, the victory against England won for them all lands and territories as far west as the Mississippi River, and the Indians would simply have to move west beyond the river.

In 1787, the United States attempted to improve relations with the passage of the Northwest Ordinance. Unfortunately, the language—"The utmost good faith shall always be observed towards the Indians; their land and property shall never be taken from them without their consent"—was not lived up to.

Fighting erupted throughout the frontier in the 1790s. Many of the veterans of the Revolutionary War fought the Indians for the rest of their lives. General Anthony Wayne, for example, defeated a large Indian force at the Battle of Fallen Timbers in 1794. Nonetheless, for the next century, as the American settlers moved westward and encroached on Indian lands, "Manifest Destiny" reined supreme over the Native Americans.

One of the little known results of the American Revolution comes from the Native American perspective and their different perception of George Washington. While most Americans refer to him as the "Father of our Country," in the Indian world he is known by his Iroquois name *Conotocarious,* which translates as "Town Destroyer."

African Americans in the American Revolution

During the Colonial era and thereafter, Africa-Americans were considered inferior and employed primarily as slaves. However, the Revolutionary War, coupled with the spirit of liberty, slowly but significantly impacted this status quo.

In fact, the years leading up to the Revolution witnessed very slow adaptations to the norms of society regarding African-Americans in particular. While American Indians were generally considered distant and dangerous savages, the status of Africans living in close proximity with whites—especially in the Northern states—slowly began to change.

Primarily in the North, where there was little need for wholesale agricultural labor, blacks were used much like white indentured servants, as domestics and general laborers. Because the colonists were deeply religious, the natural question of holding a people in perpetual bondage struck many as sinful. Accordingly, many blacks in the Northern colonies were released into society as "free blacks." One of the most illustrious examples is the Patriot poet Phillis Wheatley. (See the chapter entitled *Women in the American Revolution* for more details.)

The plight of blacks in the Southern colonies was very different. There, planters were dependent upon slaves for cheap labor. The notion of freeing their "property," which they needed for their livelihoods, was stoutly resisted. Nonetheless, beginning with Bacon's Rebellion in 1676, blacks in Virginia were offered their freedom if they voluntarily committed to military service. After hostilities ceased, the blacks were again subjected to restrictions. For several decades they were not allowed to possess firearms, for the Southern planters feared slave rebellions.

When the French and Indian War broke out in in North American in 1754 (known in Europe as the Seven Years' War, which began in 1756), some blacks were again freed to fight alongside whites. Dozens of black soldiers fought against the French and Indians for Col. George Washington. Unfortunately, once the war ended, blacks were again placed back into servitude.

A cycle of distrust, hatred, inequality, and shifting colonial values slowly began to change the concept of slavery. In 1772, the Chief Justice of the King's Bench, Lord Mansfield, declared that slavery "is so odious, that nothing can be suffered to support it." Officially, the laws of Great Britain outlawed slavery in England.

The following year, slaves in the American colonies began petitioning the courts for their freedom. Some sympathy was found in New England, but in the Southern colonies, and especially in Virginia, the planter elite held tightly to their colonial oppression of slaves. The colonial governor of Virginia disagreed with the planters and in 1775, Lord Dunmore decided to "arm all my own Negroes and receive all others that will come to me who I shall declare free." Tensions in Virginia reached a boiling point when Dunmore ordered the Royal Marines to secure the Williamsburg Magazine. Rumors of the slaves being freed in Virginia spread like wildfire, and the Virginia planters organized an armed retaliation against the royal governor. Dunmore fled to safety aboard a British warship at Yorktown.

Dunmore invited slaves to take up arms against the colonists and in short order nearly 500 blacks had joined Dunmore's Ethiopian Regiment. This sparked the Virginia Convention to declare death to all black insurrectionists. The ranks of Dunmore's Ethiopian Regiment swelled to 800 men, and their mantra was "Liberty to Slaves."

Unfortunately, smallpox decimated the ranks of the regiment and after losing a battle against the Americans at Great Bridge, Virginia, on December 9, 1776, Dunmore and his men fled the region. British Gen. Sir William Howe disagreed with Dunmore's tactics and ordered all blacks be discharged from service in the British Army.

In the newly formed Continental Army, Gen. George Washington was desperately trying to field a force to confront the British. The realities of war forced the white leaders to reconsider their position regarding blacks, who were once again allowed to serve throughout the state militias and in the Continental Line. General Washington authorized the organization of an entirely black regiment and with 250 volunteers, and the 1st Rhode Island Regiment was formed. Additionally, by August 1778, there were at least 850 black soldiers serving in the American army.

In June 1779, the British reversed their position on blacks with the Philipsburg Proclamation, in which Gen. Sir Henry Clinton declared, "every Negro who shall desert the rebel standard, full security to follow within these lines, any occupation which he shall think proper." Accordingly, thousands of slaves fled their masters seeking refuge within British lines. Serving in both the British and Hessian forces, blacks provided domestic and general labor as well as duties as soldiers (primarily in the fife and drum corps).

Blacks served with distinction in all the armies of the Revolutionary War, and while most of them remain unsung heroes, history records several interesting personalities and examples of courage. In March 1770, a free black named Crispus Attucks was one of the five civilians slaughtered during the Boston Massacre. In 1775, during the opening shots of the war at Concord Bridge, an armed slave named Prince Easterbrooks was one of the first Patriots to be wounded. He survived and served throughout the war. Prince Whipple served Gen. Washington as an aide throughout the long war and is depicted in the famous painting of the patriots crossing the Delaware River.

Another renowned black patriot was James Armistead Lafayette, a Virginia slave who enlisted in 1781 to serve under Gen. Marquis de Lafayette. Armistead was sent into the camp of Lord Cornwallis as a slave and a spy. The information he provided helped pave the way for a Patriot victory at Yorktown After the war, Armistead was commended for his actions, given his freedom, and awarded by Lafayette for his service. Armistead adopted his namesake from his former master William Armistead and Gen. Lafayette.

Another former slave, Salem Poor, enlisted with the Massachusetts Militia in 1775. Poor served with distinction in several battles, and a petition signed by his commander and other senior officers states: "A Negro called Salem Poor of Colonel Frye's regiment . . . behaved like an experienced officer, as well as an excellent soldier. It would be tedious to go into more detail regarding his heroic conduct. We only beg leave to say, in the person of this said Negro centers a brave and gallant soldier."

As the war progressed, thousands of blacks joined the armies on both sides. During the Siege of Yorktown in 1781, blacks were present in the ranks of both the Allies and the British. For many years, France and Spain had allowed blacks to serve in their armed forces. While slavery continued long after the American Revolution, African-Americans had proved their ability to fight alongside whites. Although many years would pass before slavery would end in the United States, the seeds for a future of freedom had been sown in our American Revolution.

Women of the American Revolution

In Colonial America, women could not own land or property, they could not vote, and they did not have the same rights as men. However, as evidenced on numerous occasions, the American Revolution spurred many changes that would one day serve as catalysts for change.

Despite the societal norms, roles, and impositions women experienced, many women were impressed by the spirit of revolution. Prior to the war, beginning in 1769, the "Homespun Movement" was led by women who rejected imported British goods. They refused to drink British tea and wove their own homespun textiles. Practicing domestic self-sufficiency throughout the colonies was a revolutionary concept, and the women excelled with innovative techniques to resist what they believed was active British oppression.

One example of an overt act and open resistance against the authority of the Crown was "The Edenton Tea Party." On October 25, 1774, fifty-one women in Edenton, North Carolina, led by Mrs. Penelope Baker, prepared a declaration that they would henceforth boycott English products including tea, clothing, and all other English imports. They bravely signed their names to this "revolutionary" document. While the event was ridiculed in England, colonists praised their courage. The ideas of non-importation and non-consumption eventually spurred the Sons of Liberty to strike at the British with the Boston Tea Party.

As the revolutionary movement morphed into actual war, the role of women changed. With their men away from home, women were forced to broaden their responsibilities and workloads. In addition to maintaining their homes, women helped the war effort by farming and making uniforms, blankets, flags, and soap.

Women also organized funding drives to support the war. Organizations such as the Ladies Association in Philadelphia collected donations for the cause. By the time the war ended, various women's groups had collected hundreds of thousands of dollars. In 1781, Gen. Washington wrote to Sarah Franklin Bache, the illegitimate daughter of Benjamin Franklin, thanking her for their selfless service: "Amidst the distress and sufferings of the Army, whatever sources they have arisen, it must be a consolation to our virtuous country women that they have never been accused of withholding their most zealous efforts to support the cause we are engaged in." Bache was instrumental in collecting funds and gathering and distributing dry goods and clothing for the soldiers.

As the war against Great Britain dragged on, thousands of women followed their husbands on their campaigns. General Washington referred to them as "Camp Followers." These women literally followed behind the troops as they marched from place to place, often joining with them when they camped. Many women were impoverished and had nowhere to go, so they provided direct support for their husbands and other soldiers by cooking, sewing, washing, and doing whatever they could to help the troops in the field.

Before long, the Continental Army agreed to allow women to perform the duties of soldiers—including spying on the enemy. While women were not officially authorized to serve in uniform, their indirect participation benefited greatly the cause of liberty. Likewise, the women of the Loyalists (Tory) soldiers also served their men as they fought to preserve the colonies and allegiance to King George III. Depending upon the politics and beliefs of their husbands, as the war visited communities, women were forced to make very difficult choices.

Because of inflamed passions, the law regarding treason became the first in the United States to address the rights of women, and made them subject to the death penalty—just like their male counterparts. By changing the language of statutes from "men" to "persons," women were obviously considered capable of making their own choices and suffering their own consequences. In particular, the treason statute of Massachusetts, issued in 1779, forced the wives of Loyalist men fighting the Patriots to side with the revolutionaries or forfeit their homes and belongings.

In addition to performing domestic responsibilities for the army, some women participated actively on the battlefield. Below are some of their stories.

Margaret Corbin was a "camp follower" who supported her husband, gunner John Corbin. On November 16, 1776, John was stationed with the 1st Pennsylvania Artillery and defending Fort Washington and Fort Tryon in New York (Manhattan). When Margaret's husband was killed in battle, she assumed his duties at the cannon until she too fell seriously wounded.

The British and Hessians won the battle and Margaret was taken prisoner along with the other surviving Patriots. Margaret was paroled as a wounded soldier. She never fully healed from her wounds, and in 1779 appealed to the Executive Council of Philadelphia and the Congressional Board of War for aid as a fully disabled wounded soldier. She was granted financial assistance, officially sanctioned as an injured soldier, and recognized for her brave deeds in battle. Congress granted her a pension, although the amount was rated as one-half that of a male soldier. Nonetheless, Margaret Corbin was carried on the military rolls until the end of the war in the Corps of Invalids and discharged in 1783.

History records her name as the first officially recognized female soldier, and the first to receive a pension in the United States Army. Margaret was buried at West Point Cemetery, the only female soldier of the American Revolution interred there.

Another female warrior was *Mary Hays McCauly*. She, too, served as a gunner in the Revolutionary War (which creates some confusion between her story and that of Margeret Corbin). Like her "sister in arms," Mary was also a "camp follower" assisting her husband William Hays. Mary suffered through the arduous winter at Valley Forge alongside her husband, and then followed him into the Battle at Monmouth Courthouse on June 28, 1778.

The combat at Monmouth was the largest in terms of the number of soldiers and cannons engaged on a single Revolutionary War battlefield, and probably the hottest; hundreds of men succumbed to the sweltering heat. As her husband's battery fired shell after shell, the men and guns needed water.

Mary earned the enduring nickname "Molly Pitcher" by running back and forth from a nearby spring to her husband's unit, carrying pitchers of water to quench the thirst of both man and machine. Between trips for water, Mary stopped on several occasions to render aid to the wounded. While assisting the men, she witnessed her husband fall. Mary rushed to his position, grabbed his rammer staff, and joined the fight. After the battle, General Washington issued her a warrant as a non-commissioned officer, and from that day forward she was known as "Sergeant Molly." Today, a battlefield monument honors her deeds. Her grave is honored with a cannon and a flagstaff.

In 1775, near the town of Hollis, New Hampshire, *Sarah Shattuck* and *Prudence Wright*, along with several other women, put on men's clothing, armed themselves with muskets and pitchforks, and helped in the defense of the Pepperell Bridge, a strategic location on the Nashua River.

Deborah Sampson was another woman soldier. She, however, impersonated a man and enlisted in the Fourth Massachusetts Regiment of the Continental Army as "Robert Shurtliff." Sampson concealed her obvious feminine form under bound clothing. While she was ridiculed for not needing to shave, the men attributed it to her youth.

Private Shurtliff (Sampson) participated in combat near Tarrytown, New York, where she was wounded in the leg. She tried to treat the wound herself (which never properly healed), but the pain and resultant fever forced her to seek medical aid, which in turn led to the discovery that she was a woman. Still, her service was honored and she was properly discharged on October 25, 1783. After the war, a letter submitted by Col. Paul Revere attesting to her military service resulted in her receiving recognition and a federal pension as a veteran soldier of the American Revolution.

Yet another brave woman was *Sybil Ludington*, more popularly known as the "female Paul Revere." Sybil's father was a militia commander in Patterson, New York. When he heard the British were moving against American forces at Danbury, Connecticut, Col. Ludington decided to call out the militia. On the evening of April 26, 1777, Sybil, then just sixteen years old, volunteered to ride through the night calling out the militiamen. Despite stormy weather, muddy roads, and a 40-mile route (twice as long as that ridden by Paul Revere), Sybil successfully accomplished her mission. The militia stopped the British advance at the small engagement at Ridgefield, and Sybil Ludington was officially praised by Gen. Washington. Ludington's town was renamed Ludingtonville in her honor, and today a statue honors her heroic service to her nation.

Elizabeth "Betty" Zane voluntarily hauled gunpowder to the men, helping to save Fort Henry (Virginia frontier) from Indians who supported the British. A historical marker near present-day Wheeling, West Virginia, honors her service. Coincidentally, she was an aunt of famous Western author Zane Grey, who named his own daughter Betty Zane.

Women living on the frontier faced not only the British and Tories but also attacks by Indians. In rural northern Georgia, the fabled *Nancy Hart* is renowned for both spying and fighting. Many tales have been handed down regarding the exploits of this woman who local Cherokee Indians referred to as "Wahatchee," which means "War Woman." There are so many tales surrounding her exploits that it is difficult to discern fact from fiction. However, there is no doubt that she was well-known for her frontier fighting abilities. In Georgia, there is a county, a city, a lake, and many schools and roads named in her honor.

Several women served the Patriot cause as spies and dispatch messengers. Women traveled bravely between lines as couriers and covert observers, gathering intelligence on the enemy as well as concealing secret dispatches on their person. History records women such as *Lydia Darragh, Dicey Langston, "Mom" Rinker, Eleanor Hitchcock,* and *Harriet Prudence Patterson Hall* who conducted such dangerous operations. They used many innovative and clandestine methods to deliver messages regarding enemy troop movements. Some hid dispatches in balls of yarn, others tucked them under their petticoats. Others hoisted signal flags to pass along important information. All of them served the cause of liberty with tremendous courage.

Women served in many capacities during the American Revolution, and one of the most honorable methods of service was as a nurse. General Washington realized early on how necessary nurses would be to his Medical Corps, and authorized one nurse for each ten men receiving care (due to wounds or illness). While there was no formal training for nurses, throughout history women have traditionally served in this capacity without pay. Nonetheless, Washington paid the women between two and eight dollars per month as well as a daily ration of food. Women throughout the states offered their homes and services as nurses where and when they could. An example of this selfless service is evidenced by *Margaret Hill Morris,* who transformed her home in Burlington, New Jersey, into a hospital.

Two of the most well-known women of the revolutionary era were *Abigail Adams* and *Mercy Otis Warren.* Both were prolific writers who wielded powerful words with the stroke of their quills. Both were wives of ardent Patriots (John Adams and James Warren). As evidenced in their writing, they felt a deep passion in their pleas for equal rights. While their husbands fought for liberty and struggled to establish a new country with new laws, Abigail and Mercy worked diligently to persuade their male counterparts to consider the plight of women. Despite their pleas, the 18th century world was not yet prepared to afford women their just considerations.

The women refused to give up their quest, and their eloquently written words advocate equality issues that echo the foundation of the freedoms they would never see. While John Adams and his peers in Congress were writing the foundational documents of a new nation, Abigail penned the following note to her husband: "If particular care and attention is not paid to the Ladies, we are determined to foment a rebellion, and will not hold ourselves bound by any Laws in which we have no voice or representation." As a result, John Adams wrote to James Warren, "Tell your wife that God almighty has entrusted her with the powers for the good of the world, which, in the cause of his providence, he bestows on few of the human race. That instead of being a fault to use them, it would be criminal to neglect them."

Mercy Otis Warren went on to become a published author and playwright. Early in the struggle for liberty (1772-1775), she published anonymously several popular anti-British and anti-Loyalist plays. Known as the "Conscience of the American Revolution," her pointed words left no doubt as to her literary capabilities of persuasion.

In a 1774 letter to a friend, Mercy Warren wrote, "America stands armed with resolution and virtue; but she still recoils at the idea of drawing the sword against the nation from whence she derived her origin. Yet Britain, like an unnatural parent, is ready to plunge her dagger into the bosom of her affectionate offspring."

From her incisive 1776 work entitled *The Blockheads* to her grand multi-volume history of the American Revolution entitled *History of the Rise, Progress, and Termination of the American Revolution* (1805), Warren spent much of her life following literary pursuits. Her book about the Revolution was the first non-fiction historical account of the war, and was praised highly by Thomas Jefferson.

Any list of women Patriots and talented writers would be incomplete without addressing a young black female from Boston (via Africa) named *Phillis Wheatley*. As the first published African-American woman and poet, Miss Wheatley was very popular in both the United States and England. In 1773, she was granted her freedom and her insightful words of liberty and justice are echoed in her inspirational poems. Publicly praised by Gen. Washington, John Paul Jones, and many other leading Americans for her exceptional abilities as an orator and poet, Phillis gained a large following and is still read widely today. Unfortunately, she died at the young age of thirty-one, but lives on through her writing. She is considered to be the founder of African-American literature and is honored by several monuments bearing her name and likeness.

While it would be many more years before women achieved the personal liberties they deserved, the American Revolution provided the foundation future generations of women would proudly utilize in their quest for equality.

Prisoners in the American Revolution

Some 11,500 Americans died while imprisoned during the Revolutionary War. This number is about double the number of Americans killed in battle during the same eight years (1775-1783). British and Hessian soldiers also died in captivity, though in numbers far fewer the Americans. We know today that the British intentionally mistreated American prisoners, making suffering and death a part of the Crown's plan to persuade the Americans to cease their revolt.

The Geneva Convention regarding the treatment of prisoners did not exist in the 18th century. The normal practice between warring factions and nations was that the jailers would not provide food and clothing to their prisoners of war. In other words, these supplies had to be provided by the losing side to sustain their captured troops, or the prisoners would suffer and starve. The Unites States could barely feed and clothe its own forces in the field, much less transfer aid to the British for soldiers held in prison. The fact that the British Parliament did not recognize Americans in captivity as prisoners of war with any rights (they considered them criminals guilty of treason against the Crown) only served to complicate the problem. Hanging was the common British sentence for treason, but the British knew mass hangings would add additional hatred and fan the flames of dissent in the civilian populations. As a result, the practice was avoided.

A limited practice of prisoner exchange occurred, usually in exchange for high-ranking individuals or particular exchanges for specific quantities of a particular rank. Lower ranking individuals had little hope of freedom with the exception of limited "paroles" granted on an ad hoc basis and at the leisure of the commanders in the field.

When the British lost significant numbers of troops at the major American victory at Saratoga in 1777, appeals were made regarding humane treatment of these prisoners. The situation provided the Americans with limited leverage regarding prisoner negotiations, but the status quo remained for Americans in captivity. It was not until 1782, following the surrender of the British Army at Yorktown, that British authorities finally and officially granted captured American soldiers status as Prisoners of War (POW).

For the British, maintaining many thousands of captured American soldiers on land was very difficult and resource intensive. The British solution was to use obsolete, captured, or damaged ships as floating prisons. The British could easily control the Americans, who were usually chained below decks, and thus keep them away from the eyes of the inquisitive public. The prisoners suffered terribly under appalling conditions inside the holds of these vessels, where extremes in weather, dampness, mold, contagion, and starvation took their toll. Thousands more died of neglect while imprisoned than were killed on the battlefield.

The greatest concentration of American prisoners were held in 16 vessels in Wallabout Bay just off shore from Brooklyn, New York. When the prisoners died, the British simply tossed their bodies overboard. Smaller numbers were also held in prison ships at Charleston, South Carolina, and Savannah, Georgia. Corpses that floated ashore were often retrieved by locals and buried. Although records are incomplete, at least three out of four of the prisoners held in these ships died in captivity, and the survivors never forgot their hellish experience.

The HMS *Jersey*, an aged, dismantled warship (and probably the most notorious British prison ship) housed hundreds of prisoners in terrible conditions. At its peak, the population in the *Jersey* exceeded 1,000 souls; one can only imagine the stench and heat of the summer sun baking the men within the decrepit hull. The words of a survivor best capture the sentiment of life aboard this living hell:

> Silence was a stranger to our dark abode. There were continual noises during the night. The groans of the sick and the dying; the curses poured out by the weary and exhausted upon our inhuman keepers; the restlessness caused by the suffocating heat and the confined and poisonous air, mingled with the wild and incoherent ravings of delirium, were the sounds which, every night, were raised around us in all directions. Frequently the dying, in the last mortal throes of dissolution, would throw themselves across their sick comrades, who, unable to remove the lifeless bodies, were compelled to wait until morning before they could be freed from the horrid burden. Dysentery, small-pox, yellow fever, and the recklessness of despair, soon filled the hulk with filth of the most disgusting character.

General Washington wrote frequently to British authorities regarding the vile treatment of his captured soldiers. During the course of the war, the British added the additional torture of offering the American prisoners their freedom if they would fight for England. When he learned of this choice, Washington's merciful pleas transformed into threats of retaliation. The cruelties continued, although Admiral Howe informed Washington that the rumors he heard about the conditions in the ships were exaggerations.

Too many people with firsthand knowledge of the truth made it impossible for the British to hide this from the public. A July 10, 1778, article in the *Connecticut Gazette* described life aboard the prison ships:

> They were all naked . . . Their sickly countenances and ghastly looks were truly horrible, some swearing and blaspheming, some crying, praying and wringing their hands and stalking about like ghosts, others delirious, raving and storming; some groaning and dying, all panting for breath; some dead and corrupting, air so foul at times that a lamp could not be kept burning, by reason of which the boys were not missed till they had been dead ten days. There were five or six deaths a day.

Philip Freneau, a poet, sailor, and personal friend of James Madison, was captured in battle against the British frigate *Iris*. Placed in captivity onboard the *Scorpion* in New York, he "almost suffocated with the heat and stench. . . . Between decks they lay along, struggling in the agonies of death, dying with putrid and bilious fevers, lamenting their hard fate to die at such a fatal distance from their friends; others totally insensible and yielding their last breath in all the horrors of light-headed frenzy." (Freneau, *Capture of the Aurora*, 15-41).

Some captured Americans were shipped to England, where they were imprisoned in the "black hole" of Mill and Forton Prison in Portsmouth. Dysentery, pestilence, filth, dehydration, and myriad fevers killed most of these unfortunate souls. One of these prisoners, Andrew Sherburne, wrote,

> Many are strongly tempted to pick up the grass in the yard and eat it and some pick up old bones in the yard that have been laying in the dirt a week or ten days and pound them to pieces and suck them. Some will pick up snails out of the holes in the wall and from among the grass and weeds in the yard, boil them and eat them and drink the broth . . . Our meat is very poor in general; we scarcely see a good piece once in a month" (Livesey, *Prisoners of 1776*).

While he was stationed in France as a US diplomat, Benjamin Franklin raised money for the prisoners held in England to keep them from having to "eat rats."

Like the British, the Americans also took and held prisoners. Depredations were committed on both sides, but most of the British and Hessian prisoners were secured on land and in buildings and survived their ordeal. In fact, most of these enemy soldiers were released as "parolees" because the Americans could not feed them. According to one captured British officer, "The Americans treat us very cavalierly. The provisions we are allowed are barely sufficient to subsist on. My effects, to the amount of upwards of £300 have been taken from me and the bed I lie on is a bundle of straw" (*London Chronicle*, September 2, 1777).

At war's end, surviving prisoners were released and most returned home. Thousands of Hessians, however, chose to remain in the United States. Wounds slowly healed, and while it would be a long time before military prisoner rights received international attention, many lessons about how to treat wartime captives were derived from the experience of the American Revolution.

Technology in the American Revolution

The years of the American Revolution (1775-1783) witnessed very little in the way of advancement in science and technology. However, there were a few breakthroughs that would mature into important advances for mankind worth discussing.

In the realm of military technologies, important developments employed in combat include (1) the first submarine; (2) the first breech-loading military rifle (applied with innovative maneuver warfare); and (3) biological warfare.

The First Submarine (used in battle)

Just prior to the revolution, a science student at Yale University named David Bushnell (1740-1826) experimented with underwater explosives. He created the first successful fused time bombs and developed concepts for the first submersible manned apparatus (or submarine).

Bushnell graduated from Yale in the summer of 1775 just as the world around him erupted into war with Great Britain. Spurred on by possible military applications of his innovative technologies, Bushnell spent his last dime on his submersible experiment. Because of its appearance of conjoined turtle shells, he dubbed his creation the *American Turtle*. His "submarine" was hand-constructed of watertight oak beams, driven by a hand-cranked screw propeller (a new concept), and used pumped water chambers for ballast (yet another innovation). The small single-man elliptical watercraft was also equipped with a compass and a rudimentary depth gauge. It was Benjamin Franklin who recommended these instruments use bioluminescent foxfire (naturally glowing plant) for illumination.

Franklin was excited by the prospect of using *American Turtle* as a secret weapon against the British navy. Bushnell decided he would maneuver underwater toward an enemy vessel and quietly screw a watertight "torpedo" laden with an explosive charge against the hull and then withdraw, exploding the device via a timed fuse. General George Washington provided additional financing and military assistance to complete Bushnell's audacious plan.

In theory, Bushnell's concept of operation seemed entirely possible and arrangements were commenced to employ the *American Turtle* against British ships in New York harbor. The *American Turtle* was secretly delivered to New York, but its operator would be a military man trained by Bushnell: Sergeant Ezra Lee of the Continental Army.

On September 6, 1776, Sergeant Lee bravely piloted the *American Turtle* into New York harbor just off Staten Island. Beneath the calm evening waters and under the cover of a moonlit night, he stealthily approached Sir Admiral Richard Howe's flagship HMS *Eagle*. Riding at anchor, the massive warship was an inviting and vulnerable target. Unfortunately, it had a metal-clad hull and it was impossible to attach the explosive charge. Nonetheless, Sergeant Lee detonated the charge as close as possible to the *Eagle*, although the explosion failed to damage the ship.

Another similar attempt ended prematurely when alert British seamen spotted the approaching vessel in the Hudson River. The sloop carrying the submarine to its next mission was sank by the British and the submarine slipped into the depths, ending the first experiments of submarine warfare. After the loss of his *American Turtle,* Bushnell turned his attention to a new concept: floating mines.

Floating Mines

On August 13, 1777, at Black Point Bay, Connecticut, Bushnell set adrift several mines that floated into British ships anchored in the harbor. The crew of the HMS *Cerberus* spotted the approaching mines and the ship's captain cut the rope on a mine, narrowly averting disaster. One mine, however, did destroy a small schooner.

On another occasion, Bushnell deployed floating keg mines in the Delaware River against British ships anchored near Philadelphia, Pennsylvania. Although they failed to destroy their targets, the British were extremely apprehensive about the new danger and employed sentries to watch for "torpedoes."

In August 1779, Bushnell accepted a military appointment with the rank of Captain-Lieutenant and was assigned to the US Army, Corps of Sappers and Miners (present-day Engineer Corps). On June 8, 1781, Bushnell was promoted to full Captain and participated in the Yorktown Campaign. After the war, in a letter dated September 26, 1785, George Washington wrote to

Thomas Jefferson that "Bushnell is a man of great mechanical powers, fertile in invention and a master of execution."

After the war, Bushnell moved to France for a short time before settling in Warrenton, Georgia, where he taught at the Warrenton Academy. He also practiced medicine. Bushnell, hailed as the "Father of Submarine Warfare," died in 1826 . A model of his *American Turtle* is on display at the U.S. Navy Submarine Force Museum and Library in Groton, Connecticut. For his contributions to his state and his nation the state of Georgia declared August 30, 2004, "David Bushnell Day."

Military Vaccination Program (or, Biological Warfare)

Smallpox was a mortal threat throughout the 18th century, so General George Washington established an inoculation plan for incoming recruits. The British also inoculated their soldiers and seamen against the disease.

Despite inoculation and efforts at quarantine, the disease wreaked havoc throughout the war. According to John Adams, by June 1776, smallpox was a very serious threat to the war effort and was "ten times more terrible than Britons, Canadians, and Indians together" (Becker, 420). In fact, smallpox was a scourge to nearly everyone across North America. History records that as many as 130,000 people died from the disease between 1775-1782.

On several occasions, Washington suspected that the British intentionally engaged in biological warfare by dispatching infected people into American encampments. In a December 4, 1775, letter from Washington to the President of the Congress, John Hancock, Washington claimed the British were using smallpox as "a weapon . . . against us."

During the Siege of Boston in 1775, British deserters admitted to the Americans that their commanders had ordered smallpox operations, but these accusations remain unproven. However, in 1781 during the Yorktown Campaign, a letter from British Gen. Alexander Leslie to Cornwallis states, "About 700 Negroes are come down the River in the Small Pox, I shall distribute them about the Rebel Plantations." On at least three occasions the disease significantly impacted military operations: Siege of Boston (British and American); Canadian Campaign (American), and the formation of Dunmore's Ethiopian Corps (British).

The spread of smallpox also affected civilians and Native American Indians. The tragic results of smallpox and other epidemic diseases on morale, public sentiment, and civil laws continued into the 19th century.

General Washington's decision to enforce mandatory inoculations and quarantine during the revolution likely played a key role in the establishment of future health laws and practices that eventually emerged in the United States.

The First Breech-Loading Rifle Adopted for Military Use

The "Ferguson Rifle" was named for its inventor, British military officer Maj. Patrick Ferguson (1744-1780). Ferguson created his rifle by improving the Chaumette breech-loading mechanism used in English hunting rifles. In 1776, he tested the prototype rifle at his own expense and personally displayed the weapon's capabilities to the King and the Board of Ordnance.

The .68 caliber rifle could rapidly engage multiple targets at 250 yards, which was a vast improvement over the slow-loading .75 caliber British standard infantry muzzleloading musket (popularly known as the "Brown Bess"), which had an accuracy range of 50-100 yards and could be fired about three times per minute. The Ferguson Rifle could be loaded and fired six to ten rounds each minute from any position (including the prone position), which provided the soldier with the ability to use cover and concealment, and to more quickly engage targets.

Ferguson was granted an English patent for this new military technology, and by Royal decree, 102 rifles were financed and produced through a military contract between Durs Egg arms manufacturer and the British government. Ferguson also persuaded his commanders to field these "Ferguson Rifles" to a special hand-picked unit known as "Ferguson's Rifle Corps." This special frontline unit was placed under the command of Maj. Ferguson, who took it into battle at Brandywine Creek in Pennsylvania on September 11, 1777. Thrust to the forefront of the fighting, Ferguson's Rifles performed heroically, but Ferguson and many of his men were wounded. With its ranks decimated, Gen. William Howe disbanded the elite unit, remanding the rifle and its short-lived capabilities to history.

The weapon was employed briefly by a few special light infantry forces, but most British commanders refused to adopt the rifle in the regular infantry because it would have required changes in their field formations and tactics.

After Ferguson healed from his wounds, he was promoted and deployed to the Southern Theater, where he fought alongside the infamous Lt. Col. Banastre Tarleton. Ultimately, Ferguson was killed at the Battle of King's

Mountain on October 7, 1780. He was the only British soldier on the field (he commanded a Loyalist Corps). Ironically, Ferguson died in an unconventional Indian-style assault surrounded by Southern American riflemen known as the Overmountain Men.

The rifle technology and the concept of "unconventional warfare" were ahead of their time. Had the rifle been producible in inexpensive bulk lots, and had the British been afforded time to reconsider their warfighting techniques, the war very well may have ended differently. Still, Ferguson's ideas were innovative, and variations of both the arms technology and his battlefield concepts were eventually adopted.

American Flags of the Revolution

United States of America

In 1775, the opening shots of the American Revolution were fired by New England militiamen. The banners and flags they carried depicted various symbols and slogans because there was no unifying headquarters or organizational regulations regarding them. Thus, many of the initial flags bear statements such as, "Liberty," "Hope," "Appeal to Heaven," and the more commonly known phrase, "Don't Tread on Me."

Accompanying these statements were symbols including trees, anchors, stripes, and animals and reptiles. Few of these symbols have much of a connection to modern America. In the 1770s, however, they were very significant to the locals who carried them into battle. The trees, snakes, and beavers were prevalent in colonial America, and their easy recognition reflected local connections to the land.

In short order, more politically oriented emblems became popular on the local banners. For example, the "Liberty Tree," a stately old elm in Boston where the Sons of Liberty rallied became a very popular flag in the Boston area. One of the most widely known early flags bore the rattlesnake with its famous declaration, "Don't Tread on Me." This particular flag has resurfaced in contemporary politics.

The rattlesnake and its bold statement were prominently displayed on both the "Gadsden Flag" and the "Culpeper Flag." These flags were carried by several different militia organizations in both the Northern and Southern colonies. The rattlesnake bore a powerful testament as evidenced in the *Philadelphia Journal*, a period newspaper. In 1775, these comments were published anonymously, but historians suspect they were written by Benjamin Franklin. Regarding the snake, the author states:

> The Rattle-Snake is found in no other quarter of the world besides America . . . her eye excelled in brightness that of any other animal and that she has no eye-lids. She may, therefore, be esteemed an emblem of vigilance. She never begins an attack, nor, when once engaged, ever surrenders. She is, therefore, an emblem of magnanimity and true courage. . . . She never wounds till she has generously given notice,

even to her enemy, and cautioned him against the danger of treading on her.

Another anonymously published observation reads:

> I confess I was wholly at a loss what to make of the rattles, 'till I went back and counted them and found them just thirteen, exactly the number of the Colonies united in America; and I recollected too that this was the only part of the Snake which increased in numbers. . . . Tis curious and amazing to observe how distinct and independent of each other the rattles of this animal are, and yet how firmly they are united together, so as never to be separated but by breaking them to pieces. One of those rattles singly, is incapable of producing sound, but the ringing of thirteen together, is sufficient to alarm the boldest man living.

Franklin is also known to have rejected early appeals to use the Eagle as a symbol of the independence movement. According to Franklin, the Eagle is "a bird of bad moral character."

Despite the differences in meaning and appearance, the militiamen proudly carried their individual flags into battle. The men of Rhode Island fought beneath a flag comprised of thirteen stars, a large anchor, and the word "Hope" prominently displayed on a large white field. In South Carolina, a bold blue field highlighted a crescent moon. Beneath their flag, these defenders of Fort Moultrie wore matching blue uniforms and caps emblazoned with the words "Liberty or Death." The Culpeper Minutemen of Virginia adopted the rattlesnake and same mantra of "Liberty or Death," plus the statement "Don't Tread on Me."

As the revolutionary movement grew, opinions impacted the symbols associated with resistance to the Crown. The press rallied the colonists to unite and eventually the differences merged into a unifying effort with a formal Declaration of Independence. As the individual states merged under the Continental command of Gen. George Washington, the Army, Navy, and Marines continued using individual regimental flags.

After July 4, 1776, however, as the battles and bloodshed increased, the color red achieved a more prominent place on American flag designs. Several variations of flags with red and white stripes signifying the 13 states became popular. One variant known as the Grand Union flag combined the red and white stripes with the Union Jack of Great Britain placed in the upper left corner (the canton). Others replaced the Union Jack with a centered rattlesnake and (again) the phrase "Don't Tread on Me."

On June 14, 1777, the Continental Congress announced the adoption of a national flag. The declaration of the flag's adoption states:

> Resolved: that the flag of the United States be thirteen stripes, alternate red and white; that the union be thirteen stars, white in a blue field, representing a new constellation. Stars represent Delaware (December 7, 1787), Pennsylvania (December 12, 1787), New Jersey (December 18, 1787), Georgia (January 2, 1788), Connecticut (January 9, 1788), Massachusetts (February 6, 1788), Maryland (April 28, 1788), South Carolina (May 23, 1788), New Hampshire (June 21, 1788), Virginia (June 25, 1788), New York (July 26, 1788), North Carolina (November 21, 1789), and Rhode Island (May 29, 1790).

While historians disagree as to who was responsible for the "first flag," in April of 2009, the Pennsylvania Historical and Museum Commission declared the following on a historical marker at the original Philadelphia home of Betsy Ross:

> Credited with making the first stars and stripes flag, Ross was a successful upholsterer. She produced flags for the government for over 50 years. As a skilled artisan, Ross represents the many women who supported their families during the Revolution and early Republic.

The flag attributed to her is known today as the "Star-Spangled Banner" and the "Betsy Ross" flag.

Despite the differences of the individual states, the new nation was finally joined together under one flag.

The Revolutionary War Bookshelf

By no means comprehensive, the following list aims to provide casual readers with a number of ideas for additional reading on a wide variety of Revolutionary War subjects.

General Histories

Alden, John R. *A History of the American Revolution*. New York: Alfred A. Knopf, 1972.

Boatner, Mark Mayo, III. *Encyclopedia of the American Revolution*. New York, 1966.

Ferling, John E. *Setting the World Ablaze: Washington, Adams, Jefferson and the American Revolution*. New York: Oxford University Press, 2000.

Fleming, Thomas. *Washington's Secret War: The Hidden History of Valley Forge*. Smithsonian, 2005.

Galvin, John R. *The Minute Men: The First Fight: Myths and Realities of the American Revolution*. Herndon, 2006.

Higginbotham, Don. *The War of American Independence, Military Attitudes, Policies, and Practice, 1763-87*. New York, 1971.

Lossing, Benson J. *Pictorial Field Book of the Revolution*. 2 vols. New York, 1858.

Trevelyan, George Otto, Richard B. Morris, editor. *The American Revolution*. New York, 1964.

Van Doren, Carl. *Secret History of the American Revolution*. New York, 1941.

Ward, Christopher. *The War of the Revolution*. 2 vols. New York, 1952.

Battles and Campaigns

Babits, Lawrence E. *A Devil of a Whipping: The Battle of Cowpens*. Chapel Hill, 1998.

——. *Long, Obstinate, and Bloody: The Battle of Guilford Courthouse*. Chapel Hill, 2009.

Buchanan, John. *American Revolution in the Carolinas*. New York, 1997.

——. *The Road to Guilford Courthouse: The American Revolution in the Carolinas*. New York, 1999.

Greene, Jerome A. *The Guns of Independence: The Siege of Yorktown, 1781*. New York, 2005.

Ketchum, Richard M. *Saratoga: Turning Point American Revolutionary War*. New York, 1997.

Lefkowitz, Athur S. *Benedict Arnold's Army: The 1775 American Invasion of Canada during the Revolutionary War*. New York, 2008.

Luzader, John. *Saratoga: A Military History of the Decisive Campaign of the American Revolution*. New York, 2008.

Savas, Theodore P., and Dameron, J. David. *A Guide to the Battles of the American Revolution*. New York, 2005.

Scott, John Albert. *Fort Stanwix (Fort Schuyler) and Oriskany*. Rome, New York, 1927.

Spring, Matthew H. *With Zeal and With Bayonets Only: The British Army on Campaign in North America, 1775-1783*. Norman, 2008.

Williams, John. *The Battle of Hubbardton: The American Rebels Stem the Tide*. Vermont Division of Historic Preservation, 1988.

The Armies

Berg, Fred Anderson. *Encyclopedia of Continental Army Units*. Harrisburg: Stackpole Books, 1972.

Fortesque, Sir John. *History of the British Army*. 13 vols. London, 1899-1902.

Commanders

Bass, Robert D. *The Green Dragoon: The Lives of Banastre Tarleton and Mary Robinson*. New York: Henry Holt and Co., 1957.

Higginbotham, Don, *Daniel Morgan: Revolutionary Rifleman*. Chapel Hill, 1979.

Freeman, Douglas Southall. *George Washington: A Biography*. 6 vols. New York: Charles Scribner's Sons, 1952.

Golway, Terry. *Washington's General: Nathanael Greene and the Triumph of the American Revolution*. New York, 2004.

Howson, Gerald. *Burgoyne of Saratoga: A Biography*. New York, 1979.

Knollenberg, Bernhard. *Washington and the Revolution, A Reappraisal: Gates, Conway, and the Continental Congress*. New York, 1941.

Nelson, Paul David. *General Horatio Gates: A Biography*. Baton Rouge, 1976.

Patterson, Samuel White. *Horatio Gates: Defender of American Liberties*. New York, 1941.

Randall, Willard Sterne. *Benedict Arnold: Patriot and Traitor*. New York, 1990.

Willcox, William B. *Portrait of A General: Sir Henry Clinton in the War of Independence*. New York, 1964.

The Revolutionary War on the Web

The Internet has witnessed a substantial expansion of sites dedicated to the American Revolution. Some belong to libraries and archives, many of which have shown an interest in making their holdings more accessible to the public. Others are the creations of authors, researchers, and enthusiasts who have decided to share their knowledge and findings with a wider audience. As with all things Internet-related, some sites offer outstanding, quality information, while others push nonsense, quasi-facts, and agendas.

The following brief list aims to point readers to a <u>sampling</u> of reliable and useful sites. As with all Web sites, the addresses of some may change in the coming years or stop publishing altogether. As of this writing, these sites were all active and thriving.

Libraries and Archives

Library of Congress (<u>www.loc.gov/</u>). The Web site of the nation's premier repository offers visitors a variety of opportunities for further research. Check out the Digital Collections page (<u>www.loc.gov/library/libarch-digital.html</u>) to search through select manuscript, newspaper, and map collections. For those interested in Civil War images, check out the Prints and Photographs Online Catalog (http://www.loc.gov/pictures/).

National Archives and Records Administration (<u>www.archives.gov/</u>). At first blush, the National Archives' site might be a bit intimidating—there are so many options to choose from. Not to worry: start searching by typing in Revolutionary War.

General Interest

The National Parks Service (www.nps.gov). A comprehensive list of national parks. Find information on each park's operating hours and history, obtain a copy of its brochure, and take a virtual tour!

American Revolutionary War (www.en.wikipedia.org/wiki/American_Revolutionary_War). Wikipedia is a good place for general information about the Revolution, as long as readers understand that anyone can edit the page and update it. Do not rely upon this information except as a starting point for your reading.

The American Revolutionary War (http://www.myrevolutionarywar.com/battles/index.htm). A useful site that covers battles and campaigns, documents, leaders, and politics.

The American Revolution (http://www.theamericanrevolution.org/). A general site for reading about a wide variety of topics.

Liberty! The American Revolution (http://www.pbs.org/ktca/liberty/). This is a wonderful companion interactive site that supports the PBS broadcast of a show of the same name. Test your knowledge with the Road to Revolution game!

Revolutionary War Timeline (http://www.nps.gov/archive/cowp/timeline.htm). This National Park Service website offers a helpful timeline to major events of the war, with some links to battlefield park sites.

Battles of the Revolutionary War (http://www.sonofthesouth.net/revolutionary-war/). This site offers interesting information on a wide variety of topics, as well as maps and illustrations.

Southern Campaigns of the American Revolution (http://www.southerncampaign.org/). In addition to information on battles in the Southern colonies, this website offers information and links to Revolutionary War Roundtables, where you can attend and here talks about this topic.

Revolutionary War Blogs

American Revolution and Founding Era (http://americanfounding.blogspot.com/). Offers a wide variety of information about the war and colonial America.

American Revolution Blog (http://americanrevolutionblog.blogspot.com/). Info on the Revolution, American colonization, and early american history.

British Soldiers, American Revolution (http://redcoat76.blogspot.com/). Info about British soldiers in the American Revolution.

Boston 1775 (http://boston1775.blogspot.com/). History, analysis, and unabashed gossip about the start of the American Revolution in Massachusetts.